DAY
BY
DAY
for the
Holy Souls
in Purgatory

SUSAN TASSONE

Our Sunday Visitor Publishing Division
Our Sunday Visitor, Inc.
Huntington, Indiana 46750

Nihil Obstat
Msgr. Michael Heintz, Ph.D.
Censor Librorum

Imprimatur
✠ Kevin C. Rhoades
Bishop of Fort Wayne-South Bend
August 12, 2014

The *Nihil Obstat* and *Imprimatur* are official declarations that a book is free from doctrinal or moral error. It is not implied that those who have granted the *Nihil Obstat* and *Imprimatur* agree with the contents, opinions, or statements expressed.

ISBN: 978-1-61278-772-5 (Inventory No. T1577)
RELIGION/Christian/Catholic; RELIGION/Inspirational; RELIGION/Meditations

eISBN: 978-1-61278-352-9
LCCN: 2014944886

Cover design: Amanda Falk
Cover art: Ravensburg Madonna of Mercy, by Michael Erhart,
from the image collection compiled for the ARC Museum.
Image courtesy of the Art Renewal Center® — www.artrenewal.org.
Interior design: Sherri L. Hoffman
Interior art: Photos courtesy of Susan Tassone

PRINTED IN THE UNITED STATES OF AMERICA

To Steven Jay Gross
— whose love, compassion, and wisdom are an inspiration to all
people and animals that have encountered him —
with profound thanks and gratitude.

"The Purgatory Lady"

THE MADONNA OF MERCY

Gracing the cover, the image of the Virgin, who shelters under her outspread mantle a group of the faithful in need of protection, is probably derived from one of the provisions of medieval law. This conferred on women of high rank the privilege of granting to persecuted people who call upon their aid the "protection of the mantle" — safe refuge and freedom from persecution. This theme is found in theological literature from the early thirteenth century and emerged as a devotional image in the late thirteenth century. The famous Madonna of Mercy in the Berlin sculpture collection, originally attributed by art historians to the Ravensburg sculptor Friedrich Schramm, is now unanimously considered to be the work of Michael Erhart of Ulm.

Mary Most Holy Liberates Souls

*"O daughter, you are blessed by the Most High God
above all women on earth." — Judith 13:18*

Sister Paula of St. Teresa, a Dominican, relates that one Saturday when she had been rapt into ecstasy and transported into purgatory, she was amazed to see that prison transformed into a paradise of delights, with radiance flooding its center, where thick darkness usually prevailed. Sister Paula beheld the Virgin encircled by a throng of angels. To each angel she gave the command to liberate and lead to heaven certain souls who had been especially devoted to her in life.

Reflection: Glory be to you, who are ever ready to assist us in life and death! Lead us to the kingdom of heaven! Rejoice, O Virgin Mary; rejoice a thousand times! Glory be to the Father, and to the Son, and to the Holy Spirit. As it was in the beginning, is now, and ever shall be, world without end. Amen.

---

*Eternal rest grant unto them, O Lord, and let perpetual
light shine upon them. May they rest in peace. Amen.*

FOREWORD

Susan Tassone begins with the Catholic teaching that the souls of people who had faith and love for God and for neighbor but died in an imperfect moral and spiritual state could still be perfected after death in purgatory. Though they are "assured of their eternal salvation," they still need to "undergo purification" that makes possible "the holiness necessary to enter the joy of heaven" (*Catechism of the Catholic Church*, n. 1030). These souls cannot earn any merits in purgatory but suffer passively there. Still, the prayers and works of the living can bring them merit and benefit (CCC, n. 1032).

The next point permeates her whole book: we pray for the souls in purgatory simply because they need our prayers. A selfless Christian love for these suffering souls, whether we knew them in life or not, is the primary motive for praying, fasting, helping the needy in works of charity, and offering up suffering all for the relief of the pain these souls experience in purgatory. Frequently, the reflections in the book remind us that these souls undergo painful torment during their time of purification, a suffering that is primarily due to the absence of the direct experience of God's love. As truly redeemed souls, they know that infinite love awaits their cleansing that makes their ability to receive that love possible, and missing that love is the source of their pain. The passages chosen for each day of the year in this book evoke sympathy from the readers on a daily basis as they reflect on the insights of the saints, popes, Fathers of the Church, and mystics. Then, as we, the members of the Church still living on earth, offer our small sacrifices for them, they already experience various touches of love in purgatory, especially when Holy Mass is offered for their intention and they experience the death and resurrection of Jesus Christ as the true source and power of the love we offer for their sake.

There are certain true gains for those who pray for the poor suffering souls in purgatory, to be sure. On one level, we make great spiritual progress by praying for the souls of people who have offended and hurt us in the past. This comes from a general principle that it is very difficult

to remain angry with people who have caused you hurt, or whom you resent, or upon whom you seek revenge when you pray for them. Prayer simply dissolves the anger, resentment, and revenge, if you are willing to take that step. This certainly applies to the living, and it seems to apply to those who have died. Therefore, praying for the dead souls who caused us pain and suffering in the past evokes a new sympathy for them, a tender acceptance of their faults and failings, widens our ability to love them, and leads to deeper love for them. Not only will prayer for the souls of the dead increase our love for them, but it will free us to love God more truly and love the rest of our fellow sinners in this life.

A benefit in praying for the poor souls is that our deepening love for them, despite the foibles and moral weaknesses that got them to purgatory, may also make us more aware of our own need in this life to pursue greater righteousness and holiness so that we can avoid purgatory. Prayer for those suffering on account of their venial sins and for the temporal punishment due to forgiven sins may well motivate us to move away from unreflectively accepting sin in our lives toward a thirst for greater moral integrity and sanctity.

Another benefit of this book comes from the daily insights into the theology of purgatory. Little has been taught on this topic in seminaries, schools, or pulpits, making this compilation of texts by popes, councils, saints, and Fathers of the Church a useful source on the Church's constant teaching on the doctrine of purgatory. Meditation on the daily passages from Scripture and the reflections will strengthen a Catholic mind on this teaching, in addition to evoking a deepened love for the poor souls. This may well awaken a love of the faith and its truth, an ever-greater love of God and neighbor, a firmer desire to avoid hell and the sins that lead one there, and a hope and desire for the eternal bliss and beauty of existing with the good God in heaven for all eternity, directly experiencing his infinite love.

Read this book prayerfully, and let us pray for each other that "we may ... cheerfully meet in heaven" (St. Thomas More's words to those who condemned him to death).

— FATHER MITCH PACWA, S.J.

PERSONAL
ACKNOWLEDGMENTS

Our Sunday Visitor Publishing conducted a survey of their readers and found that purgatory was one of the most asked-about topics. For more than a decade, Our Sunday Visitor has given me the honor and privilege to address this mysterious yet consoling doctrine, the good news and hope of purgatory.

I have had the outstanding support of Our Sunday Visitor, under the leadership of Greg Erlandson, president of the publishing division. My editor, Jackie Lindsey, with her tremendous support (our eighth book together), led the way to opening doors for the suffering souls. Her commitment to this project made it the magnificent work that it is today. Bill Dodds, award-winning novelist, did an award-winning job as copyeditor — and I also thank my constant champion project editor since 2003, George Foster. John Christensen, national sales and advertising director, shared with me the excitement and enthusiasm for this book expressed by one of the leading book distributers in the world. I share the title of "leader of the purgatory movement in the world" with these incredible professionals.

No one walks alone on life's journey. Special thanks and gratitude to Joseph Pronechen, Catholic journalist, for following the "Purgatory Lady" over the years, writing many outstanding articles about my works that share the plight of the suffering souls. To Michael Wick, Institute on Religious Life, creative colleague extraordinaire, who is always willing to share his innovative ideas. To Father Joe McCabe, Maryknoll Missionary, for his constant support in promoting the purgatory message to our bishops and nuncios worldwide. To Father Scott Haynes, S.J.C., who put a face on purgatory with the classics of Shakespeare, for his insights into Scripture and poetic writings, and translations from Latin. And a

repeated heartfelt thanks to Steven Jay Gross, my friend, to whom this book is dedicated.

To EWTN's president, Doug Keck, and producer Lee South. EWTN is the voice that carries the cry of the suffering souls all over the world. A thousand cheers from the holy souls.

To you, my readers: I have walked into many churches and adoration chapels around the country and the world and found you praying for the holy souls with our purgatory books. I climbed rugged mountain terrains with the Stations of the Cross and found you in prayer with our *Way of the Cross for the Holy Souls in Purgatory*. Our purgatory books are found on bookshelves in Marian shrines in Europe, England, Ireland, the Philippines, Australia, and Croatia, to name just a few. It gives me great joy to see this devotion spreading and to chat with you and hear your personal stories. Keep on praying. We must empty purgatory!

Finally, to all the purgatory authors worldwide, past and present: This book would have not been possible without them unlocking the mystery of purgatory.

Praise God forever!

INTRODUCTION

God Is Inviting You

The more I learn about purgatory, the more I come to realize this God-given gift isn't about punishment. It's about love.

It's where our merciful Father helps the holy souls prepare to be with Him, face-to-face, for all eternity.

And, amazingly, our beloved Father invites us to help them, too. We on earth — through our prayers, sufferings, sacrifices, and acts of kindness offered to God on behalf of those souls — can help speed them on their way home.

A few suggestions on how you can use this book:

- Continue your vigil for the holy souls as a yearlong novena.
- Follow the seasons of the year.
- Pray the book by choosing a favorite month.
- Pray with the Church throughout the liturgical year.
- Carry it with you and pray.
- Open the book randomly and pray, picking a page as the Spirit leads you!

God bless you today and always. You, and the souls of all your dear ones, are in my prayers.

— SUSAN

WINTER

During this time of year, when nature is dormant and the silence of winter surrounds you, think about the silent voices of the souls in purgatory.

Holy Angels, guardians of those blazing chasms, help me to call to mind those souls, so holy and resigned, from the bowels of the flames that torment them. Make us recognize among them our fathers, our mothers, our sisters, and brothers. Let their cries, so tender and heart-rending, capable of splitting the mountains and mollifying cruelty itself, reach and penetrate our ears.

— Father Charles Arminjon

TABLE OF CONTENTS

God and the Eternal Marriage Feast

*The marriage of the Lamb has come, and his Bride
has made herself ready. — Revelation 19:7*

"This early Jewish idea of an intermediate state includes the view that these souls are not simply in a sort of temporary custody but ... are already being punished or are experiencing a provisional form of bliss. There is also the idea that this state can involve purification and healing which mature the soul for communion with God.

"The early Church took up these concepts, and in the Western Church they gradually developed into the doctrine of Purgatory.... For the great majority of people — we may suppose — there remains in the depths of their being an ultimate interior openness to truth, to love, to God. In the concrete choices of life, however, it is covered over by ever new compromises with evil — much filth covers purity, but the thirst for purity remains and it still constantly re-emerges from all that is base and remains present in the soul. What happens to such individuals when they appear before the Judge? Will all the impurity they have amassed through life suddenly cease to matter? What else might occur? ... [I]t is in any case evident that our salvation can take different forms, that some of what is built may be burned down, that in order to be saved we personally have to pass through 'fire' so as to become fully open to receiving God and able to take our place at the table of the eternal marriage-feast" — Pope Benedict XVI, (*Spe Salvi*, nn. 45-46).

Reflection: Make acts of love so we may burn away our faults.

---

*Eternal rest grant unto them, O Lord, and let perpetual
light shine upon them. May they rest in peace. Amen.*

In the Silences of God

*It is good that one should wait quietly for the
salvation of the LORD. — Lamentations 3:26*

"Suffering all these things, the soul undergoes its purgatory; for the attributes of God arise and make war within the soul which sees its natural darkness as opposed to light, its poverty, misery, and malice in contrast to the riches and goodness of God, until the flame succeeds in purifying the soul and, while transforming it, enriches, glorifies, and delights.

"And this great work of God — the work of purgatory — is done in the silences of God, in the silence of created things, in the silence of truth, in the silence of perfect trust. Let us think for a moment about one of these silences.

"Silence of trust: If we knew God, nothing could trouble us any more. At their judgment, the holy souls receive so great an illumination of soul that they know, as it were, God. Blessed should we be if we could believe in a like proportion!" — St. John of the Cross.

Reflection: Let your mind picture each of the silences mentioned by St. John of the Cross.

---

*Eternal rest grant unto them, O Lord, and let perpetual
light shine upon them. May they rest in peace. Amen.*

Four Fruits

*What does the L*ORD *require of you but to do justice, and to love
kindness, and to walk humbly with your God. — Micah 6:8*

"Every one of our good works, every act that we do for God in a state of
grace, may have four kinds of fruit: a fruit of *merit*, a fruit of *propitiation
(to appease)*, a fruit of *impetration (to beg a favor)* and a fruit of *expiation* or
to make amends, or *satisfaction* so that the faithful soul which does such a
work may by the same prayer ask and obtain a favor, appease the wrath of
God, merit an increase of grace on earth, increases its glory in heaven, and
satisfy the justice of God by expiating its sins" — Father Martin Jugie,
Assumptionist, Byzantine scholar, author.

Reflection: One of the best ways of doing penance is to multiply
your works of charity and mercy toward the dead, which wipes out
your own debt to God's justice.

---

*Eternal rest grant unto them, O Lord, and let perpetual
light shine upon them. May they rest in peace. Amen.*

Evangelizers of the Holy Souls

Do the work of an evangelist, fulfill your ministry. — 2 Timothy 4:5

"I was in purgatory tonight. It was as if I were being led into an abyss, where I saw a large hall. It is touching to see the poor souls so quiet and sad. Yet their faces reveal that they have joy in their hearts, because of their recollection of God's loving mercy. On a glorious throne, I saw the Blessed Virgin, more beautiful than I had ever beheld her. She said: 'I entreat you to instruct people to pray for the suffering souls in purgatory, for they certainly will pray much for us out of gratitude. Prayer for these holy souls is very pleasing to God because it enables them to see Him sooner'" — Revelations of Blessed Anne Catherine Emmerich.

Reflection: Do all you can to spread devotion to the holy souls in purgatory.

Eternal rest grant unto them, O Lord, and let perpetual light shine upon them. May they rest in peace. Amen.

Christ's Gaze of Love

"Lift up the light of thy countenance upon us, O LORD!" — *Psalm 4:6*

"Willingly would we suffer twice the torment we now endure, willingly would we suffer until judgment day, if only we could see Jesus gazing on us with love" — A soul to St. Margaret Mary.

Reflection: Make an act of desire for the holy souls to see God: Eternal Father, turn Your merciful gaze upon all mankind and especially sinners, all enfolded in the most compassionate heart of Jesus. For the sake of His sorrowful passion show us Your mercy, that we may praise the omnipotence of Your mercy forever and ever. Amen.

Eternal rest grant unto them, O Lord, and let perpetual light shine upon them. May they rest in peace. Amen.

Open the Gates of Purgatory

Incline thy ear to me, rescue me speedily. — *Psalm 31:2*

"The soul is cleansed by purgatorial pains after death, and in order that they may be rescued from their pain, they are benefited by the suffrages of the living faithful, namely: the Sacrifice of the Mass, prayers, alms, and other works of piety" — St. Jerome.

Reflection: The love of the Church for her departed children reaches out as the grand gift giver of Christ's merits and riches and is powerful to assist them. From the beginning the Church has honored the memory of the dead. This teaching is based on the practice of prayer for the dead, already mentioned in Sacred Scripture. Stretch out your hand in compassion for these prisoners of love.

Eternal rest grant unto them, O Lord, and let perpetual light shine upon them. May they rest in peace. Amen.

Remember Me at the Altar of the Lord

"Do this in remembrance of me." — Luke 22:19

"Lay this body wherever it may be. Let no care of it disturb you: this only I ask of you, that you should remember me at the altar of the Lord wherever you may be" — St. Monica, on her deathbed, to her son St. Augustine.

Reflection: St. Augustine says: "Recognize in this bread what hung on the Cross, and in this chalice what flowed from His side." Whom do you miss the most, whom do you wish you could have done more for? Have a Mass offered for them! Ask the heavenly Father every time you attend Mass to grant you a holy death — to die in the state of grace — and to avoid purgatory.

Eternal rest grant unto them, O Lord, and let perpetual light shine upon them. May they rest in peace. Amen.

Month's Mind

For the living know they will die, but the dead know nothing, and they have no more reward; but the memory of them is lost. — Ecclesiastes 9:5

"St. Peter used every day to exhort the faithful to be careful to give decent burial to the dead, to pray and obtain the prayers of others for the repose of their souls; so high a value did he attach to that work of charity and so anxious was he that the living should help the souls which were languishing.... Let the third day after death be consecrated by the recitation of psalms, lessons, and prayers for the love of Him who rose again on the third day; and let the same be done on the ninth and thirtieth day according to ancient usage. Lastly, let us celebrate the anniversary in memory of the deceased person, and let alms be distributed in his name" — Pope Clement IV.

Reflection: Triple your fervor with the offering of Memorial Masses.

Eternal rest grant unto them, O Lord, and let perpetual light shine upon them. May they rest in peace. Amen.

The Power of Gregorian Masses

He drew me up from the desolate pit. — Psalm 40:2

Pope St. Gregory had a fervent devotion for purgatorial souls, so much so that he lamented that after his death he would not be able to assist them. Tradition holds that Our Lord spoke to him and said: "My friend, I want to grant in your favor a privilege that will be unique. All souls in purgatory, for whom thirty Masses are offered in your honor and without interruption, will immediately be saved however great may be their debt toward me." St. Gregory popularized Gregorian Masses, a series of thirty Masses celebrated on thirty consecutive days. It is related in the *Dialogues of St. Gregory* that the soul of a departed monk appeared and declared that he had been delivered from purgatory upon completion of thirty Masses. The Church does not officially declare a soul is released from purgatory but points to the efficacy of the Mass.

Reflection: Arrange to put Gregorian Masses in your wills. They are the greatest gift you can give yourself and your beloved dead.

Eternal rest grant unto them, O Lord, and let perpetual light shine upon them. May they rest in peace. Amen.

Sanctifying Grace

My heart is steadfast, O God, my heart is steadfast! — Psalm 57:7

"A living person is still capable of growing in sanctifying grace. A Mass offered for a person already in God's grace has the effect of offering a gift of increased grace which the person may willingly receive in order to become more Christ-like.

"A Mass offered for a person in the state of mortal sin may yet supply the grace necessary for repentance even though the conversion is always a free acceptance of the grace that is offered" — Father Edward McNamara, Legionary of Christ, professor of liturgy, Angelicum University, Rome.

Reflection: Offer a Mass for yourself while you are alive and one for every year of your life.

Eternal rest grant unto them, O Lord, and let perpetual light shine upon them. May they rest in peace. Amen.

Consolation of Almsgiving

Blessed is he who considers the poor! The LORD delivers
him in the day of trouble. — Psalm 41:1

"Throughout Holy Scripture, the value of almsgiving is exalted. With alms one relieves so many miseries, and consoles so many unfortunates — children, orphans, the sick, the aged, the poor. Two advantages follow, therefore: charity toward the needy and charity toward the suffering souls in purgatory" — Blessed James Alberione, Italian priest, founder of the Daughters of St. Paul and the Society of St. Paul, author.

Reflection: Take every opportunity to help those whom God puts in your life and those around you who are in need, for the sake of the suffering souls.

Eternal rest grant unto them, O Lord, and let perpetual
light shine upon them. May they rest in peace. Amen.

A Heavenly Deposit

"Where your treasure is, there will your heart be also." — Matthew 6:21

"Jewish beggars in history addressed their prospective patrons with the words *zeki bi*, literally meaning 'acquire a merit through me' or rephrased: 'make a deposit to your heavenly treasure through me.' In speaking this way they were simply repeating a common tradition that had already appeared in the Books of Sirach and Tobit. The idea of a 'heavenly bank' was born, and along with it the idea that making a deposit to this bank was like making a loan to God" — Gary A. Anderson, professor of theology, author.

Reflection: Give up something that is dear to you in life on behalf of the holy souls.

Eternal rest grant unto them, O Lord, and let perpetual light shine upon them. May they rest in peace. Amen.

JANUARY 14

Suffering for Charity's Sake

If I give away all I have, and if I deliver my body to be burned, yet do not have charity, it profits nothing. — *1 Corinthians 13:3*

"The gift that a man makes of his good works and indulgences for the souls in purgatory multiplies their merits a hundredfold in the sight of God. 'When a man suffers for another for charity's sake, the satisfaction or the penance that he offers is more pleasing to God than if he offered it for Himself'" — St. Thomas Aquinas.

Reflection: Blessed Paul VI states in his *Apostolic Constitution on Indulgences* (nn. 8, 10): "And if the faithful offer indulgences in suffrage for the dead, they cultivate charity in an excellent way and while raising their minds to heaven, they bring a wiser order into the things of this world.... [I]n fact by means of indulgences members of the Church who are undergoing purification are united more speedily to those of the Church in heaven." Make little sacrifices for others. Keep little sufferings between you and Jesus.

Eternal rest grant unto them, O Lord, and let perpetual light shine upon them. May they rest in peace. Amen.

Grace Molds Us

Teach us to number our days that we may get
a heart of wisdom. — Psalm 90:12

"Few souls understand what God would accomplish in them if they were to allow His grace to mold them according to His will. Would it not be terrible after the sufferings and trials of this life to still have to suffer in purgatory?" — St. Ignatius of Loyola.

Reflection: Allow God's grace to mold you. Pray to understand the Father's will and His love for you.

Eternal rest grant unto them, O Lord, and let perpetual
light shine upon them. May they rest in peace. Amen.

JANUARY 16

God Flows in These Souls

*The peace of God, which passes all understanding, will keep your
hearts and your minds in Christ Jesus. — Philippians 4:7*

"Souls in purgatory unite great joy with great suffering. One does not
diminish the other ... and day-by-day this happiness grows as God flows
in these souls, more and more the hindrance to His entrance is consumed.
The hindrance is the rust of sin and the fire burns the rust away so that
more and more the soul opens itself to the divine inflowing.... No peace
is comparable to that of the souls in purgatory except that of the saints in
heaven. On the other hand, the souls in purgatory endure torments which
no tongue can describe and no intelligence comprehend, without special
revelation" — St. Catherine of Genoa.

Reflection: Meditate on the joys and sufferings of purgatory.

---

*Eternal rest grant unto them, O Lord, and let perpetual
light shine upon them. May they rest in peace. Amen.*

Enraptured in Ecstasy

What no eye has seen, nor ear heard, nor the heart of man conceived,
what God has prepared for those who love him. — 1 Corinthians 2:9

"St. Catherine of Siena one day was enraptured in ecstasy and saw the mysteries of God the Most High. Once the vision ended, she realized that she was still living here on earth. She became inconsolable. She sobbed in desolation: 'I thought I was in heaven forever, yet I find myself to be still here below!' Beloved souls in purgatory, you see God, yet you are still in prison. Poor souls, poor souls! I hear you exclaim: 'Oh, Father, Oh, Father!' and then I see you suffering in anguish" — St. Louis Guanella, founder of the Pious Union of St. Joseph in 1924.

Reflection: Ask a friend to join you in praying for the holy souls and remember them in your prayer groups.

Eternal rest grant unto them, O Lord, and let perpetual
light shine upon them. May they rest in peace. Amen.

A Second Chance?

*It is appointed for man to die once, and after
that comes judgment. — Hebrews 9:27*

Purgatory is not where people go for a "second chance." It's only for those whom God has destined for heaven and for those who die in the state of grace. The *Catechism of the Catholic Church* teaches us: "Death is the end of man's earthly pilgrimage, of the time of grace and mercy which God offers him so as to work out his earthly life in keeping with the divine plan and to decide his ultimate destiny" (n. 1013).

And: "Death puts an end to human life as the time open to either accepting or rejecting the divine grace manifested in Christ. The New Testament speaks of judgment primarily in its aspect of the final encounter with Christ in his second coming, but also repeatedly affirms that each will be rewarded immediately after death in accordance with his works and faith" (n. 1021).

Reflection: Petition God to help you live and die in the state of grace for all your family members.

---

*Eternal rest grant unto them, O Lord, and let perpetual
light shine upon them. May they rest in peace. Amen.*

Overcoming Self-Centeredness

*"If you would be perfect, go, sell what you possess
and give to the poor, and you will have treasure in
heaven; and come, follow me." — Matthew 19:21*

"Purgatory says that God does not regard this failure as final. He does not come to us and say, 'You've failed me completely. Enough! I am through with you!' Rather he comes to help us complete the work we've left undone....

"Purgatory is not a chamber of horrors. It is a place where shallowness and selfishness are overcome. It is a time of spiritual growth and maturing. It infallibly leads to the Beatific Vision of God....

"If he were to put people in heaven selfish, unprepared, and spiritually immature, it could not really be heaven for them. It is in full giving of self that one receives the fullness of God's love" — Father Michael J. Taylor, S.J., Scripture scholar, author.

Reflection: Accept all trials as a means to fulfill your debt to God.

---

*Eternal rest grant unto them, O Lord, and let perpetual
light shine upon them. May they rest in peace. Amen.*

JANUARY 20

Lest We Forget the Departed

He who closes his ear to the cry of the poor will himself cry out and not be heard. — Proverbs: 21:13

"Those who in this life forget the departed will be in my opinion, deprived in purgatory of all participation in good works and devout prayers, though ever so many be offered up for them by others. The faithful, however, who do not forget the suffering souls completely, but seldom think of them, will not be deprived of friends and intercessors entirely, but will derive very little help and comfort, and their complaints will be answered by the words of St. Paul: 'He who sows sparingly, shall reap sparingly' (2 Cor 9:6)" — St. Cajetan.

Reflection: At the Consecration of the Mass, lift up these mournful souls.

Eternal rest grant unto them, O Lord, and let perpetual light shine upon them. May they rest in peace. Amen.

Fidelity to Grace

*The Lord disciplines him who he loves, and chastises
every son whom he receives. — Hebrews 12:6*

One New Year's Day St. Margaret Mary Alacoque prayed earnestly for three deceased persons. Two were religious and the third secular. Our Lord showed all three to her, saying: "Which one do you wish to give Me?" The saint humbling herself entreated Our Lord to make the choice Himself according to His greater glory and good pleasure. Then He delivered the soul of the secular, saying that He had less compassion for the religious, because even though they had more means of meriting and expiating their daily faults during life, they had been unfaithful to the practice of their rule.

Reflection: Practice fidelity to the inspirations of grace, to atone for the infidelity of deceased souls.

---

*Eternal rest grant unto them, O Lord, and let perpetual
light shine upon them. May they rest in peace. Amen.*

Purgatory as Process

Nothing unclean shall enter it. — Revelation 21:27

"In following the Gospel exhortation to be perfect like the heavenly Father (cf. Mt 5:48) during our earthly life, we are called to grow in love, to be sound and flawless before God the Father 'at the coming of our Lord Jesus with all his saints' (1 Thess 3:12f.). Moreover we are invited to 'cleanse ourselves from every defilement of body and spirit' (2 Cor 7:1; cf. 1 Jn 3:3), because the encounter with God requires absolute purity.

"Every trace of attachment to evil must be eliminated, every imperfection of the soul corrected. Purification must be complete, and indeed this is precisely what it means on the Church's teaching on *purgatory*. The term does not indicate a place, but a condition of existence" — St. John Paul II (General Audience, August 4, 1999).

Reflection: Pick one vice you find in your life and work to erase it for the day.

Eternal rest grant unto them, O Lord, and let perpetual light shine upon them. May they rest in peace. Amen.

Lamentations

*"Have pity on me, O you my friends, for the
hand of God has touched me." — Job 19:21*

"I am full of bitterness and saturated with anguish, and my eyes are blinded with weeping. Who will deliver me from this prison of pain? I have left on earth parents, children, friends, and they have all forgotten me, while I am paying for the zeal which I labored for their temporal welfare. I denied myself even the necessities of life, I shortened my sleep. I neglected my religious duties to work for them. Ungrateful ones, what evil have I done you that you should treat me like this?

"I have given up everything for you, and you say not a single prayer for me. Did you not promise when you stood sobbing at my deathbed? Such were not the hopes you held out to me when you pressed my failing hands in a last farewell. The hand of God is heavy upon me and I am tormented in this pain" — The Voice of a Forgotten Soul.

Reflection: St. Leonard of Port Maurice states: "They [the holy souls] have a right to complain, for little has been given them." Are we listening? Do we have time for these holy sufferers? We must make time for them. Do many acts of kindness today in the name of the holy souls. Let us not be deaf to the cries of the forgotten ones.

---

*Eternal rest grant unto them, O Lord, and let perpetual
light shine upon them. May they rest in peace. Amen.*

Saints and Souls — An Unbreakable Bond

"There is no one who has left house or brothers or sisters or mother or father or lands, for my sake and for the gospel, who will not receive a hundredfold now in this time." — Mark 10:29-30

"The Church, in her most profound truth, is *communion* with God, intimacy with God, a communion of love with Christ and with the Father in the Holy Spirit, which extends to brotherly communion. This relationship between Jesus and the Father is the 'matrix' of the bond between us Christians: if we are intimately part of this 'matrix,' this fiery furnace of love, then we can truly become of one single heart and one single soul among us. For God's love burns away our selfishness, our prejudices, our interior and exterior divisions. The love of God even burns away our sins....

"[T]he communion of saints goes *beyond earthly life, beyond death and endures for ever.* This union among us goes beyond and continues in the next life; it is a spiritual communion born in Baptism and not broken by death, but, thanks to the Risen Christ, is destined to find its fullness in eternal life. There is a deep and indissoluble bond between those who are still pilgrims in this world — us — and those who have crossed the threshold of death and entered eternity. All baptized persons here on earth, the souls in Purgatory and all the blessed who are already in Paradise make one great Family. This communion between earth and heaven is realized especially in intercessory prayer" — Pope Francis (General Audience, October, 30, 2013).

Reflection: Let us strengthen the bond we have between us and the holy souls. Keep constant remembrance of them throughout the day.

Eternal rest grant unto them, O Lord, and let perpetual light shine upon them. May they rest in peace. Amen.

Complacent Christians

"And do you not remember?" — *Mark 8:18*

"Remember that when a priest stands up in front of the assembly and announces that so-and-so is in heaven, it sends a message that says, 'Why pray for his soul? He's in heaven.' And if the deceased, like my friend, was lapsed from the faith, canonizing the person communicates the message that doing your own thing will give you a fast track ticket to heaven. It also implies that everyone goes to heaven! That's a dangerous thought. But, this is just where the devil wants us. He loves complacent Christians. He wants us to believe that getting to heaven is easy. He also wants us to believe that the souls in purgatory don't need our prayers. He's cunning and sly, subtle and manipulative. He hates God, he hates us, he hates the Church. He uses his time wisely and sets his snare with great care. So why are we giving him so much room to maneuver?" — Peggy Frye, convert from an evangelical church, Catholic apologist.

Reflection: If you loved them in life, love them in death with your prayers. Remember those who had an elaborate funeral, but who have no relief in their pain.

Eternal rest grant unto them, O Lord, and let perpetual light shine upon them. May they rest in peace. Amen.

Interior Delight of the Souls

*I am sure he who began a good work in you will bring it
to completion at the day of Jesus Christ.* — *Philippians 1:6*

"Just as the pains of purgatory are severe, so the interior satisfaction and
bliss enjoyed by the souls there must surpass anything we can imagine.
How wonderful it must be for them when they feel themselves gradually
being spiritually healed, gradually being freed from their remaining moral
debt to God, and gradually drawing nearer and nearer to the joyful vision
of the Blessed Trinity!" — St. Francis de Sales.

Reflection: Pray: Jesus, meek and humble of heart, make my heart
like unto Thine.

---

*Eternal rest grant unto them, O Lord, and let perpetual
light shine upon them. May they rest in peace. Amen.*

JANUARY 27

O Blessed Purgatory ... A Time of Maturing

*Bring me out of prison, that I may give
thanks to thy name! — Psalm 142:7*

"Pain and joy exist together in these souls who are undergoing a time of purification before entering paradise. This 'time' must not be understood literally. Strictly speaking there are no days or hours in the life to come. It is a matter of progress, of development, a 'spiritual time' in Jean Guitton's words [a Catholic philosopher, theologian and author], a matter of quality not quantity. They are happy at being saved, unhappy at being held back and having to delay. Freed from the burden of matter, they are, all to God, all in God, all for God" — Redemptorist Fathers Maurice and Louis Becque, French authors.

Reflection: Ask a young person to pray with you for the holy souls.

*Eternal rest grant unto them, O Lord, and let perpetual
light shine upon them. May they rest in peace. Amen.*

Victorious Intercessors

"But you, take courage! Do not let your hands be weak, for your work shall be rewarded." — 2 Chronicles 15:7

"A man of great virtue, when approaching his end, was violently assaulted by evil spirits surrounding his deathbed. Suddenly he saw the heavens opening and thousands of warriors in white garments coming to his aid. They told him that they were sent to defend and to gain victory for him. The dying man was greatly relieved and implored his heavenly defenders to tell him who they were. They replied: 'We are the souls whom you released. We come to reward your charity and to conduct you to heaven'" — Venerable Cardinal Cesare Baronius, ecclesiastical historian, author.

Reflection: The holy souls feel an urgency to assist their relatives and friends. Their gratitude is unbounded. Thank God for their prayers.

Eternal rest grant unto them, O Lord, and let perpetual light shine upon them. May they rest in peace. Amen.

Patron Saints in Action

*Here is a call for the endurance of the saints, those who keep the
commandments of God and the faith of Jesus. — Revelation 14:12*

"The holy patrons whose names we have born, and who have protected
us during life, continue their assistance to their clients who groan in the
flames of purgatory.

"Numberless patron saints are personally interested in multitudes of
souls. The affectionate relation between their clients and themselves not
only subsists, but a deeper tenderness has entered into it because of the
accomplished victory. They see in the holy souls their own handiwork,
the fruit of their example, the answer to their prayers, the success of their
patronage, the beautiful and finished crown of their affectionate intercession" — Father Frederick Faber, convert, English hymn writer, theologian, author.

Reflection: Open yourself to imitate your patron saint as an example.

---

*Eternal rest grant unto them, O Lord, and let perpetual
light shine upon them. May they rest in peace. Amen.*

Gifts from the Grateful Souls

"Praise God and give thanks to him; exalt him and give thanks to him in the presence of all the living for what he has done for you." — Tobit 12:6

"These destitute, suffering souls do not wait until they enter heaven to exhibit their gratitude towards their benefactors: while they still languish in purgatory, they pray without intermission for the welfare of soul and body, obtain for them recovery from disease, assistance in poverty, help in necessities, counsel and protection on journeys and in danger, preservation and increase of their temporal goods, aid them in the salvation of their souls, and, above all, come to their relief in the agonies of death and before the judgment seat of God" — Bishop Joseph Colmar of Mainz, Germany.

Reflection: In all your needs take refuge in the charitable souls.

Eternal rest grant unto them, O Lord, and let perpetual light shine upon them. May they rest in peace. Amen.

St. Gertrude's Heroic Act of Charity

With God we shall do valiantly. — Psalm 60:12

St. Gertrude was tempted by the devil at the hour of death. Our Lord reminded her that she offered all her merits for the dead. But not content with sending His angels and the thousands of souls she released to assist her, Our Lord said He would take her straight to heaven and multiply a hundredfold all her merits.

The Heroic Act is a beautiful and effective offering to God for the souls in purgatory of all works of satisfaction and suffrages we may gain during life: "O Holy and Adorable Trinity, desiring to cooperate in the deliverance of the souls in purgatory, and to testify to my devotion to the Blessed Virgin Mary, I secede and renounce, in behalf of the holy souls, all the satisfactory value of all my works during life, and all the suffrages which may be given to me after my death, consigning them entirely into the hands of the Blessed Virgin Mary, that she may apply them according to her good pleasure to the souls of the faithful departed, whom she desires to deliver from their sufferings. Deign, O my God, to accept and bless this offering I make to You at this moment. Amen."

Reflection: Do all you can to make known the Heroic Act. Pray for those who make this act.

---

*Eternal rest grant unto them, O Lord, and let perpetual
light shine upon them. May they rest in peace. Amen.*

Hungry Souls in Purgatory

*"I am the bread of life; he who comes
to me shall not hunger." — John 6:35*

"Let us imagine that in the whole world there was but one bread and that it could satisfy the hunger of all. Just to look at it would be to nourish oneself.

"That bread is what a healthy man, with an appetite, would seek; and when he could not find it or eat it, his hunger would increase indefinitely. Aware that that bread alone could assuage his hunger, he would also know that without it his hunger could never abate.

"Such is the hell of the hungry who, the closer they come to this bread, the more they are aware that they do not as yet have it. Their yearning for that bread increases, because that is their joy. Were they to know that they would never see the bread, that would be perfect hell, the case of the damned souls who no longer hope to see the true bread and the true God.

"The hungry souls in purgatory, however, though they do not see as much of the bread as they would wish, hope to see it and fully enjoy it one day. This, then, is their suffering, the waiting for the Bread that will take away their hunger" — St. Catherine of Genoa.

Reflection: Give food to your local food pantry for the sake of the hungry souls.

---

*Eternal rest grant unto them, O Lord, and let perpetual
light shine upon them. May they rest in peace. Amen.*

Never Stop Praying for Your Dead

If one member suffers, all suffer together; if one member is
honored, all rejoice together. — 1 Corinthians 12:26

"One night, a sister who had died two months previously came to me ... in a terrible condition ... her face terribly distorted.... I redoubled my prayers for her. The next night she came again, but I saw her in an even more horrible state.... I asked, 'Haven't my prayers helped you?' She answered that my prayers had not helped her and that nothing would help her.... I replied, 'If my prayers are not helping you, Sister, please stop coming to me.' She disappeared at once. Despite this, I kept on praying.... She came back again ... and her face was radiant, her eyes beaming with joy. She told me I had true love for my neighbor and that many other souls had profited from my prayers. She urged me not to cease praying for the souls in purgatory, and she added that she herself would not remain there much longer. How astounding are the decrees of God!" — St. Faustina (*Diary*, 58).

Reflection: Be persistent in prayer, as it shows your love of neighbor.

Eternal rest grant unto them, O Lord, and let perpetual
light shine upon them. May they rest in peace. Amen.

The Need for Prayer

I am not aware of anything against myself, but I am not thereby acquitted. It is the Lord who judges me. — 1 Corinthians 4:4

"These good souls with all their glorifying me, will make me languish in purgatory, for they will imagine that I have no need of prayer. Behold what such reputation will profit me" — St. Francis de Sales, speaking of those who sang his praises.

Reflection: We tend to stop praying for our departed too quickly. How often during the year do you pray for your deceased loved ones?

Eternal rest grant unto them, O Lord, and let perpetual light shine upon them. May they rest in peace. Amen.

FEBRUARY 4

Love Never Ends

Remember those who are in prison, as though
in prison with them. — *Hebrews 13:3*

"I have loved this prince [Theodosius], and because, I have loved him, I shall not leave him until I have led him into that abode to which his virtues call him. O people, hasten here and, together with me, bestow upon the remains of this prince the incense of your prayers, the outpourings of your charity, and the grief of your penance" — St. Ambrose.

Reflection: In his encyclical *Spe Salvi*, Pope Benedict XVI wrote: "No man is an island, entire of itself. Our lives are involved with one another, through innumerable interactions they are linked together. No one lives alone. No one sins alone. No one is saved alone. The lives of others continually spill over into mine in what I think, say, do and achieve. And conversely, my life spills over into that of others: for better or for worse. So my prayer for another is not something extraneous to that person, something external, not even after death. In the interconnectedness of Being, my gratitude to the other — my prayer for him — can play a certain part in his purification" (n 48). Tell one person that you love him or her.

Eternal rest grant unto them, O Lord, and let perpetual
light shine upon them. May they rest in peace. Amen.

On the Wings of Prayers

I do not mean that others should be eased and you burdened, but that as a matter of equality your abundance at the present time should supply their want, so that their abundance may supply your want, that there may be equality. — *2 Corinthians 8:13-14*

"Our prayers for them [the holy souls] are capable not only of helping them, but also of making their intercession for us effective" — *Catechism of the Catholic Church* (n. 958).

Reflection: The greater and more intense the torment of the holy souls, the greater and stronger their gratitude. Realize the power and privilege God has given you to release the holy souls.

Eternal rest grant unto them, O Lord, and let perpetual light shine upon them. May they rest in peace. Amen.

Purgatory, Ripe for Harvest

"Truly, truly, I say to you, unless a grain of wheat falls into the earth and dies, it remains alone; but if it dies, it bears much fruit." — John 12:24

"Priests are made desolate sometimes by a sense of frustration in their ministry. It would be a source of great encouragement if they remember that the dead are always accessible and wholly responsive to their zeal. Let them turn their eyes from the discouragements about their feet, and look on purgatory as a huge field white for the harvest" — Father Martin Jugie, Assumptionist, Byzantine scholar, author.

Reflection: Pray for the priests in your life, those living and deceased. Remember deacons, too!

Eternal rest grant unto them, O Lord, and let perpetual light shine upon them. May they rest in peace. Amen.

From the Mouth of a Child

"You are the light of the world.... Let your light shine so before
men, that they may see your good works and give glory to
your Father who is in heaven." — Matthew 5:14, 16

Long ago a ray of this sublime understanding was given to a little girl chasing butterflies in the summer fields. Awestruck and wondering, she paused, and after a long halt called to her little companions and said: "Do you know what I am thinking of?" She explained: "If one of our friends was imprisoned in a house of fire, how we should rush to her help. Then how we should try to deliver the souls in purgatory."

Deliverance from purgatory means the greater glory of God. We must give Him these souls whom He is calling. That child was Blessed Mother Mary of Providence, foundress of the Helpers of the Holy Souls.

Reflection: Blessed Mary of Providence repeats: "Behold I come ... to work all my life, by prayer, by suffering and by labor for the deliverance of the souls in purgatory. My God, may I burn with love for you!" Start a Purgatorial Society in your parish.

Eternal rest grant unto them, O Lord, and let perpetual
light shine upon them. May they rest in peace. Amen.

Sins Forgotten

"I will remember their sins no more." — *Hebrews 8:12*

Purgatory is not a place of lamenting sins. According to St. Catherine of Genoa, focusing on past sins would be a form of imperfection. As such, "They cannot turn their thoughts back to themselves, nor can they say, 'Such sins I have committed for which I deserve to be here,' nor, 'I would that I had not committed them for then I would go now to Paradise,' nor, 'That one will leave sooner than I,' nor, 'I will leave sooner than he.'"

Therefore, after having seen its sins and imperfections upon death, the soul no more considers them. From here on out, the object of the soul's vision and orientation is the beauty and glory of God.

Reflection: Praise the beauty and glory of God.

Eternal rest grant unto them, O Lord, and let perpetual light shine upon them. May they rest in peace. Amen.

Never Too Late

"He is not God of the dead, but of the living." — *Matthew 22:32*

"For God is all present: for him our prayer and the death of the person for whom we are praying coincide: for him the human being whom we love and whose decision we want to make easier by the support of our prayer is dying at the moment we are praying for him.... Our intercession therefore can never arrive 'too late' since God by his very nature knows no before and after. Our aid to the deceased person always arrives at the right moment, even if we are praying for him decades after his death.

"His moment is always simultaneously our moment. His decision always occurs now, even if he long ago attained eternal bliss. At every moment of our time we can sustain him in the greatest decision of his life" — Father Ladislaus Boros, S.J., theologian, author.

Reflection: Be eager to offer Masses for members of your family tree. If possible, offer Gregorian Masses.

Eternal rest grant unto them, O Lord, and let perpetual
light shine upon them. May they rest in peace. Amen.

Purgatory Roots

For if he were not expecting that those who had fallen would rise again, it would have been superfluous and foolish to pray for the dead. But if he was looking to the splendid reward that is laid up for those who fall asleep in godliness, it was a holy and pious thought. — 2 Maccabees 12:44

In the Old Testament is the story about the Jewish general Judas Maccabeus, who came upon a field where he found many Jewish soldiers slain after a battle. Judas Maccabeus and his soldiers mourned their fellow soldiers. However, they noticed many fallen comrades wearing amulets of the false gods. In reparation, Judas Maccabeus collected two thousand silver drachmas from his soldiers, which he sent to the Temple in Jerusalem to provide for an expiatory sacrifice. Here we find the biblical foundation for our tradition of offering the expiatory Sacrifice of the Mass for the faithful departed.

Reflection: Praying for the dead is firmly rooted in Judaism. Let forgiveness take root in you. Remember our faithful departed and offer them the spiritual assistance of the Holy Sacrifice of the Mass, as we ask God's mercy for them.

Eternal rest grant unto them, O Lord, and let perpetual light shine upon them. May they rest in peace. Amen.

Say Yes to God

"Let what you say be simply 'Yes.'" — *Matthew 5:37*

St. Bernadette's "private notes" reveal: "The more I contemplate God, the more God looks on me. The more I pray to him, the more he thinks of me too."

And, she wrote, her chaplain Father Douce said: "'You must carry your cross hidden in your heart as Mary did.' Resolution: I will be joyful when I go to the parlor [convent living room], even if my heart is full of sadness. I shall say yes to God: Yes, I will go there on the condition that you free a soul from purgatory or convert a sinner."

Reflection: May your "Yes" to God be forever.

Eternal rest grant unto them, O Lord, and let perpetual light shine upon them. May they rest in peace. Amen.

Retouching Souls With His Cross

*Blessed are they who wash their robes, that they may
have the right to the tree of life.* — *Revelation 22:14*

"Take away purgatory, and God could not pardon so easily, for will an act
of contrition at the edge of the tomb atone for thirty years of sinning? Take
away purgatory and the infinite Justice of God would have to reject from
heaven those who resolve to pay their debts, but have not yet paid the last
farthing. Purgatory is where the love of God tempers the justice of God,
for there God pardons because He has time to retouch these souls with
His Cross, to recut them with the chisel of suffering, that they might fit
into the great spiritual edifice of the heavenly Jerusalem, to plunge them
into that purifying place where they might wash their stained baptismal
robes to be fit to enter into the spotless purity of heaven; to resurrect them
like the Phoenix of old from the ashes of their own sufferings so that, like
wounded eagles healed by the magic touch of God's cleansing flames, they
might mount heavenward to the city of the pure where Christ is King and
Mary is Queen, for, regardless of how trivial the fault, God cannot pardon
without tears, and there are no tears in heaven" — Venerable Archbishop
Fulton J. Sheen.

Reflection: Recite the *Te Deum* (page 393) in thanksgiving to God
for the mercy of purgatory.

---

*Eternal rest grant unto them, O Lord, and let perpetual
light shine upon them. May they rest in peace. Amen.*

Offer It Up

Count it all joy, my brethren, when you meet various trials, for you know that the testing of your faith produces steadfastness. — James 1:2

"There used to be a form of devotion — perhaps less practiced today but quite widespread not long ago — that included the idea of 'offering up' the minor daily hardships that continually strike at us like irritating 'jabs,' thereby giving them a meaning.... What does it mean to offer something up? Those who did so were convinced that they could insert these little annoyances into Christ's great 'com-passion' so that they somehow became part of the treasury of compassion so greatly needed by the human race.... Maybe we should consider whether it might be judicious to revive this practice ourselves" — Pope Benedict XVI (*Spe Salvi*, n. 40).

Reflection: Perform an act of self-denial.

Eternal rest grant unto them, O Lord, and let perpetual light shine upon them. May they rest in peace. Amen.

Selfless Lovers

For God so loved the world that he gave his only Son. — *John 3:16*

"Heaven is a place for selfless lovers; only they can be at home there. Thus, some 'purgatorial' schooling in the art of loving selflessly seems a reasonable expectation for those who die lacking a maturity in this kind of love. Though they are delayed for a time in the intermediate state, these souls are all destined for heaven. There is no despair or bitterness here. Like Advent, the process is grounded in hope; it is a time of anticipated joy" — Father Michael J. Taylor, S.J., Scripture scholar, author.

Reflection: Are you "maturing" spiritually or simply growing old?

Eternal rest grant unto them, O Lord, and let perpetual light shine upon them. May they rest in peace. Amen.

Reparation Through the Holy Face

Thou hast said, "Seek ye my face." My heart says to thee, "Thy face, LORD, do I seek." Hide not thy face from me. — *Psalm 27:8-9*

"Part of the Devotion to the Holy Face was brought to the world through a series of private revelations to Sister Marie of St. Peter, a discalced Carmelite nun of Tours, France. The devotion is one of reparation, and in one of her visions, Christ told Sister Marie that he would purify the souls at their death of those who defended His cause in this work of reparation" — Ann Ball, author.

Reflection: Prayer to the Holy Face: "Eternal Father, I offer Thee the adorable Face of Thy Beloved Son Jesus for the honor and glory of Thy Name, for the conversion of sinners and the salvation of the dying."

Eternal rest grant unto them, O Lord, and let perpetual light shine upon them. May they rest in peace. Amen.

Transformed by Holy Communion

*"I am the living bread which came down from heaven; if any
one eats of this bread, he will live forever." — John 6:51*

"If our love were ardent enough to overcome all obstacles and prepare
for Communion as the purification of purgatory prepares for the Beatific
Vision, the effects would be nearly the same. Saturated with Eucharistic life,
earthly pilgrims would be transformed in God by Holy Communion as are
the elect in glory" — M. V. Bernadot, O.P., Dominican priest, author.

Reflection: Practice reverence in receiving Holy Communion in
expiation for the suffering souls for their own faults in prayer. Pray
with St. Josemaría Escrivá before receiving Holy Communion: "I
wish my Lord, to receive You with the purity, humility, and devotion with which Your most holy mother received you, with the
spirit and fervor of the saints."

---

*Eternal rest grant unto them, O Lord, and let perpetual
light shine upon them. May they rest in peace. Amen.*

Cleansing by Pain

"Do not fear what you are about to suffer." — Revelation 2:10

"It would seem that there is no more efficacious way of cleansing self of self-love than pain accepted as the work of God. Were it not necessary, we know it would not be inflicted. Suffering frees the soul from the fascination of all that is not God; it draws away the veils of self-delusion, so that in the desert of the soul there is no oasis but God and the stream of living water which is in Him.

"And purgatory is a place where souls suffer" — Mother Mary of St. Austin, Helpers of the Holy Souls, author.

Reflection: Give up sin for the day.

Eternal rest grant unto them, O Lord, and let perpetual light shine upon them. May they rest in peace. Amen.

Souls That Shine

"Those who are wise shall shine like the brightness of the firmament; and those who turn many to righteousness, like the stars for ever and ever." — Daniel 12:3

As the soul travels to heaven — as if by the speed of light — God's consuming fire of love is infused into it. As the shades of sin recede, the soul begins to shine brighter, resembling — little by little — the splendor of God. The Book of Wisdom provides the following illustration of these justified souls: "[L]ike gold in the furnace he tried them, and like a sacrificial burnt offering he accepted them. In the time of their visitation they will shine forth, and will run like sparks through the stubble" (Wis 3:6-7).

Reflection: Pray for those souls who are closest to heaven.

Eternal rest grant unto them, O Lord, and let perpetual light shine upon them. May they rest in peace. Amen.

Chalice of His Sorrows

"He who loves his life loses it, and he who hates his life in this world will keep it for eternal life." — *John 12:25*

"Our Lord has many ready to share his table but few to partake of his sorrows, and it is for us to be among those few, if we would be in the number of his friends. Let us help him to drink his chalice for that will show that we love him sincerely. It is no easy matter to be the friend of Jesus Christ. Suffering borne for him is the only sure way to test which is the true and which the false friend. Although the draught may be bitter, yet drink it — think for whom you take it; how soon its taste will pass away; what a reward it will bring you, and it will taste so sweet that you will complain that there is so little given you. Learn to love God as he loves you, and know that a true love will make you give yourself wholly to him, and keep back nothing for yourself. Do not fear to place yourself in God's hands, abandoning yourself entirely to him, for all he holds is safe, and all else will certainly be lost" — St. John of Ávila.

Reflection: Imitate the surrender of the holy souls to relieve them.

Eternal rest grant unto them, O Lord, and let perpetual light shine upon them. May they rest in peace. Amen.

Release by Photo

*For to this you have been called, because Christ also
suffered for you, leaving you an example, that you
should follow in his steps. — 1 Peter 2:21*

Blessed Mother Teresa of Calcutta did not like having her picture taken.
She told Jesus she would offer this up if every time the camera flashed He
would release a soul from purgatory.

Reflection: Whenever you view a photo of a deceased relative, whisper a prayer for his or her soul.

*Eternal rest grant unto them, O Lord, and let perpetual
light shine upon them. May they rest in peace. Amen.*

A Price to Pay

*And all Israel heard of the judgment which the king had rendered;
and they stood in awe of the king, because they perceived that the
wisdom of God was in him, to render justice.* — *1 Kings 3:28*

"How dearly we shall pay for all those faults that we look upon as nothing at all, like those little lies that we tell to amuse ourselves, those little scandals, the despising of the graces which God gives us at every moment, those little murmurings in the difficulties that He sends us!" — St. John Vianney.

Reflection: For twenty-four hours do not complain about anything.

---

*Eternal rest grant unto them, O Lord, and let perpetual
light shine upon them. May they rest in peace. Amen.*

A Royal Escort to Heaven

*Therefore be imitators of God, as beloved children. And
walk in love, as Christ loved us and gave himself up for us, a
fragrant offering and sacrifice to God. — Ephesians 5:1-2*

Struck by the sight of her companion in sin murdered, Margaret of Cortona was converted and became a saint. She developed a tender devotion to the suffering souls and offered all her mortifications and troubles for their delivery. When she was on her deathbed, she saw an army of souls that had been delivered from purgatory forming an honor guard, a royal escort to heaven.

Reflection: Picture yourself meeting the heirs of heaven you released from purgatory.

*Eternal rest grant unto them, O Lord, and let perpetual
light shine upon them. May they rest in peace. Amen.*

One Thousand Favors

Bless the LORD, O my soul, and forget not all his benefits, who forgives all your iniquity, who heals all your diseases, who redeems your life from the Pit, who crowns you with steadfast love and mercy, who satisfies you with good as long as you live so that your youth is renewed like the eagle's. — Psalm 103:2-5.

"Though the Holy Souls cannot merit for themselves, they can obtain for us great graces. Through the sweet providence of God, they can obtain for us outstanding favors, and deliver us from evils, sickness and dangers of every kind" — St. Alphonsus Liguori.

Reflection: Petition the holy souls for a pure and charitable heart. Ask them to renew your heart with the gifts of the Holy Spirit: wisdom, understanding, counsel, fortitude, knowledge, piety, and fear of the Lord. When you have the Holy Spirit, you have everything.

Eternal rest grant unto them, O Lord, and let perpetual light shine upon them. May they rest in peace. Amen.

Implore Suffrages

*Bring me out of prison, that I may give
thanks to thy name! — Psalm 142:7*

One night while St. Paul of the Cross was preparing to retire, he heard repeated knocking at the door of his cell. It was the soul of a priest who had died a quarter of an hour earlier, coming to implore suffrages (Masses, prayers, or acts of piety). "Oh, how I suffer!" he said. "It seems to me that I have been in this ocean of fire for a thousand years!" Moved to tears, the saint arose and looking at the clock asked, "But how can it be? You have been dead only a quarter of an hour, and already it seems to you that you have spent a thousand years there?" The soul replied, "Oh, if you knew how long time is in purgatory." The soul did not withdraw until it had received a solemn promise of suffrages.

Reflection: Surrender your own desires for the release of the purgatorial souls.

*Eternal rest grant unto them, O Lord, and let perpetual
light shine upon them. May they rest in peace. Amen.*

Most Blissful Suffering

Wash me thoroughly from my iniquity, and
cleanse me from my sin! — Psalm 51:2

"Purgatory: perhaps the deepest but also the most blissful kind of suffering. The terrible torture of having to settle now all the things we have dreaded a whole life long. The doors we have frantically held shut are now torn open. But all the while this knowledge: now for the first time I *will* be able to do it — that ultimate thing in me, that total thing. Now I can feel my wings growing; now I am fully becoming myself" — Father Hans Urs von Balthasar, Swiss theologian, author.

Reflection: It has been said, "*Confess as if it were your first, last, and only time.*" Go to confession monthly. You must be in the state of grace to help the souls in purgatory.

Eternal rest grant unto them, O Lord, and let perpetual
light shine upon them. May they rest in peace. Amen.

Blessed Mother, Consoler of the Afflicted

*"Make your request, my mother; for I
will not refuse you."* — 1 Kings 2:20

"Through Mary's intercession, many souls are in paradise who would not be there had she not interceded for them." — St. Thomas Aquinas

---

Reflection: This most kind mother is not satisfied with just assisting her children. She wishes to see them out of the prison of purgatory. She offers to her Son her merits, and to the heavenly Father the merits of her Son, so the sufferings of her servants may be made lighter and shorter. Pray this fourteenth-century hymn, "Languishing in Purgatory": "You are the fount, open-wide, who washes away our blame. You assist all souls — rejecting none: Extend your hand to the dead, who continually languish in pain, O Mary!"

---

*Eternal rest grant unto them, O Lord, and let perpetual
light shine upon them. May they rest in peace. Amen.*

Use Your Riches for Good

"Make friends for yourselves by means of unrighteous mammon, so that when it fails they may receive you into the eternal habitations." — Luke 16:9

"How many are there among you who, after a dissipated, disorderly life, have lost even the courage to make amends, and the will to repent? Who shudder at the thought when their soul will stand before the gaze of the Sovereign Judge? There is an easy way to obtain mercy.... Obtain for yourselves, with that gold which has served as the instrument of so many evil passions, the support and protection of the holy souls in purgatory" — Father Charles Arminjon, French preacher, author.

Reflection: Donate something you own and value to charity.

Eternal rest grant unto them, O Lord, and let perpetual light shine upon them. May they rest in peace. Amen.

Souls Are Assured of Their Salvation

*Having been disciplined a little, they will receive great good, because
God tested them and found them worthy of himself. — Wisdom 3:5*

"The souls in purgatory are certain of their salvation, know the state of
their soul, are confirmed in good, and love the merciful God. All this
affords them great relief in their suffering. Their knowledge of the infinite
holiness of God and of their own unworthiness to behold God is great,
and prompts them to bear their sufferings willingly and with utter aban-
donment to the will of God, since these sufferings are the means of their
purification and satisfaction for their sins. Moved by contrition the souls
in purgatory would rather not go to heaven than stand before God without their wedding garments. They cannot help themselves, and their only
relief is God's mercy which awakens the Christians on earth to make sacrifices for them" — Blessed Michael Sopoćko, Polish professor of pastoral
theology, author (wrote the first brochure on Divine Mercy).

Reflection: Volunteer an hour of your time to help someone.

---

*Eternal rest grant unto them, O Lord, and let perpetual
light shine upon them. May they rest in peace. Amen.*

Like the Dewfall

Above him stood the seraphim; each had six wings: with two he covered his face, and with two he covered his feet, and with two he flew. And one called to another and said: "Holy, holy, holy is the LORD of hosts; the whole earth is full of his glory." — Isaiah 6:2-3

The angels hover around the altar at Mass to receive in golden chalices the Precious Blood of Jesus Christ in order to sprinkle it like cooling dew over the holy souls in purgatory; and every moment souls purified by this expiatory outpouring take their flight to heaven.

Reflection: The Seraphim are the first choir in the hierarchy of angels. They are known as the "fiery or burning ones." They burn eternally from their love and zeal for God. The intensity of their adoration and pure love of God pours out of them. Offer your Mass or holy hour to the Seraphim. Ask them to increase your zeal and love for God.

Eternal rest grant unto them, O Lord, and let perpetual light shine upon them. May they rest in peace. Amen.

SPRING

Purgatory is the Great Vigil, the watch kept in the twilight before the Feast of Feasts.

Holy Angels, guardians of those blazing chasms, help me to call to mind those souls, so holy and resigned, from the bowels of the flames that torment them. Make us recognize among them our fathers, our mothers, our sisters, and brothers. Let their cries, so tender and heart-rending, capable of splitting the mountains and mollifying cruelty itself, reach and penetrate our ears.

— Father Charles Arminjon

Crowns of Love

Give graciously to all the living, and withhold
not kindness from the dead. — Sirach 7:33

"God showed [a woman] purgatory's terrible cleansing fire, and the many sinners whose torments were equal to the number of their sins. Her spirit was so moved by such suffering that she seized all purgatory in her arms. She endured all the suffering, but asked Love to help her. Then God spoke: 'Do not hurt yourself by carrying a burden too heavy for you.' Her spirit replied sadly: 'Lord, I pray that you will set some free.' He said: 'How many would you like me to free?' She said: 'As many of those for whom, by your mercy, I may make atonement.' Our Lord said: 'Take a thousand souls.'

"Then the poor creatures raised themselves out of purgatory, and they were burned, bleeding, and dirty. The spirit spoke: 'Lord, what will happen to these creatures now? For they cannot enter our kingdom in this awful state.' Then in his mercy God spoke a comforting word: 'You shall bathe them in the tears of love that flow from your eyes.' All at once they saw a great basin. The unhappy beings dove into it and bathed in Love as bright as the sun. The spirit felt inexpressible joy and said: 'All creatures will praise you forever. Now these are fit to enter your kingdom.' Our Lord bent down from on high and placed on their heads the crown of Love which had redeemed them and said: 'You shall wear the crown forever so all in my kingdom will know that you have been released by tears of love nine years before your proper time'" — St. Mechthild of Magdeburg.

Reflection: Imitate the graciousness of God.

Eternal rest grant unto them, O Lord, and let perpetual
light shine upon them. May they rest in peace. Amen.

MARCH 2

Souls' Greatest Torment

*As a hart longs for flowing streams, so longs
my soul for thee, O God. — Psalm 42:1*

"... [The next night] I saw my Guardian Angel, who ordered me to follow him. In a moment I was in a misty place full of fire in which there was a great crowd of suffering souls. They were praying fervently, but to no avail, for themselves; only we can come to their aid. The flames which were burning them did not touch me at all. My Guardian Angel did not leave me for an instant. I asked these souls what their greatest suffering was. They answered me in one voice that their greatest torment was longing for God. I saw Our Lady visiting the souls in purgatory. The souls call her 'The Star of the Sea.' She brings them refreshment. I wanted to talk with them some more, but my Guardian Angel beckoned me to leave. We went out of that prison of suffering. [I heard an interior voice] which said, My mercy does not want this, but justice demands it. Since that time, I am in closer communion with the suffering souls" — St. Faustina (*Diary*, 20).

Reflection: Reflect on the sufferings of the holy souls as shown in the vision of St. Faustina.

*Eternal rest grant unto them, O Lord, and let perpetual
light shine upon them. May they rest in peace. Amen.*

MARCH 3

The Ebb and Flow of Purgatory

In the waves of the sea ... I have gotten a possession. — Sirach 24:6

"The pains of purgatory are called waves, because they are transitory, unlike the pains of hell, which never end; and they are called waves of the sea, because they are so bitter. The clients of Mary, thus suffering, are often visited and relieved by her" — St. Bernardine of Siena.

Reflection: Our Lady descends into that sea of suffering to quench the flames for the holy captives. Pray the *Memorare* (page 392) to Our Lady for these holy prisoners.

Eternal rest grant unto them, O Lord, and let perpetual
light shine upon them. May they rest in peace. Amen.

Tears of Penance

How long, O LORD? Wilt thou forget me for ever? — Psalm 13:1

"St. Augustine said: 'Our hearts are restless, until they rest in Thee, O Lord.' The souls in purgatory understand perfectly the truth of these words because their longing for the beatific vision creates intense pain. St. Teresa Ávila wrote: 'The pain of loss or the privation of the sight of God exceeds all the most excruciating sufferings we can imagine, because the souls urged on towards God as to the center of their aspiration, are continually repulsed by His justice. Picture to yourself a shipwrecked mariner, who after having long battled with the waves, comes at last within reach of the shore, only to find himself constantly thrust back by an invisible hand. What torturing agonies! Yet those of the souls in purgatory are a thousand times greater" — Father James B. Buckley, Priestly Fraternity of St. Peter, author.

Reflection: All our lives, there is a sense of someone, some One, who is missing. Our entire lives we yearn for that missing piece, a piece/ peace that can only be found in God. The closer we are to God, the more there is strength and joy — my life has direction. When we wander or ignore God, there is an emptiness, chaos, a nagging discontent. Offer all your prayers and good works today for the desolate souls.

Eternal rest grant unto them, O Lord, and let perpetual light shine upon them. May they rest in peace. Amen.

Fasting for Souls

Try to learn what is pleasing to the Lord. — *Ephesians 5:10*

To appease God's anger and obtain His mercy for the sins committed against the Lord, Moses observed a fast for forty days and nights. We are invited to follow Moses and fast and pray for the relief of the suffering souls. Fasting shows solidarity with them. They are not alone or forgotten. Fasting also persuades others to help them.

Reflection: Pray with St. John Chrysostom: "Do you fast? Give me proof of it by your works. If you see a poor man, take pity on him. If you see a friend being honored, do not envy him.

"Do not let only your mouth fast, but also the eye and the ear and the feet and the hands and all members of our bodies.

"Let the hands fast, by being free of avarice. Let the feet fast, by ceasing to run after sin. Let the eyes fast, by disciplining them not to glare at that which is sinful.

"Let the ear fast, by not listening to evil talk and gossip. Let the mouth fast from foul words and unjust criticism. For what good is it if we abstain from birds and fishes but bite and devour our brothers? May He who came to the world to save sinners strengthen us to complete the fast with humility, have mercy on us and save us. May the grace of God be with you in everything you do."

Eternal rest grant unto them, O Lord, and let perpetual light shine upon them. May they rest in peace. Amen.

Fiery Love of God

"Did not our hearts burn within us while he talked to us on the road, while he opened to us the scriptures?" — *Luke 24:32*

"The Lord your God is a consuming fire. In truth, the fire which is God consumes, to be sure, but it does not destroy. It burns sweetly. It leaves one desolate unto bliss" — St. Bernard.

Reflection: The prophet Daniel talks about God's throne being encircled in flames. "His throne was fiery flames, its wheels were burning fire" (Dan 7:9). There is a fire that burns in the Sacred Heart of Jesus; His heart burns for love of us. The Immaculate Heart of Mary burns for love of us. They love us more than anybody else and more than anybody can. When we die we are drawn into this consuming fire of love. Pray for a greater understanding of the heavenly Father's love for you.

Eternal rest grant unto them, O Lord, and let perpetual light shine upon them. May they rest in peace. Amen.

Do Your Purgatory on Earth

*"We must work the works of him who sent me, while it is
still day; night comes, when no one can work." — John 9:4*

"Let us not desire delights, daughters; we are well-off here; the bad inn
lasts for only a night. Let us praise God; let us force ourselves to do penance in this life. How sweet will be the death of one who has done penance for all his sins, of one who won't have to go to purgatory! Even from
here below you can begin to enjoy glory!

"As long as we have not reached this state, Sisters, let us beseech God
that if therefore we are to receive sufferings, they will be received here
below" — St. Teresa of Ávila.

Reflection: Review your life to determine if you have any debt
unpaid or any promise unfulfilled.

---

*Eternal rest grant unto them, O Lord, and let perpetual
light shine upon them. May they rest in peace. Amen.*

MARCH 8

Make Their Desire Your Desire

"Sir, I have no man to put me into the pool." — John 5:6

"Once the soul leaves the body it has but one desire — to unite itself to God, the only One worth loving, toward Whom it is drawn like a piece of iron by a powerful magnet. For now it knows how good God is and what joy it is to be with Him. Yet it cannot" — Blessed James Alberione, Italian priest, founder of the Daughters of St. Paul and the Society of St. Paul, author.

Reflection: The holy souls tremble and weep for assistance. Plead to the Savior for their release.

Eternal rest grant unto them, O Lord, and let perpetual light shine upon them. May they rest in peace. Amen.

The Mercies of God

I have swept away your transgressions like a cloud, and your sins like mist; return to me, for I have redeemed you. — Isaiah 44:22

"St. Gertrude had long prayed for the soul of a person whose friends were in great anxiety about his salvation, and had asked for her prayers; and one day Our Lord appeared to her and said: 'For love of you, Gertrude, I will have pity on this soul and a million others; by that Divine light which penetrates the future, I knew that you would pray for this poor man's soul, and for the sake of those future prayers I placed him, when he was in his agony, in the proper disposition to procure him a good death, and prepared him to enjoy the fruits of your charity; his soul is saved and if you desire it, I will release it from its sufferings' " — St. Gertrude.

Reflection: Offer a Mass for all future generations for the graces necessary for salvation.

Eternal rest grant unto them, O Lord, and let perpetual light shine upon them. May they rest in peace. Amen.

God Never Refuses the Holy Souls

First of all then, I urge that supplications, prayers, intercessions, and thanksgivings be made for all men. — 1 Timothy 2:1

Friar Pellegrino, a fellow friar of St. Nicholas of Tolentino, had recently died.

Pellegrino brought St. Nicholas to purgatory. He saw souls of every age experiencing tremendous pain. Pellegrino said to St. Nicholas: "Behold the state of those who sent me to you. Since you are agreeable in the sight of God, we have confidence that He will refuse nothing to the oblation of the Sacrifice offered by you, and that His Divine Mercy will deliver us."

Reflection: Imagine the pain of the souls. Pray for those whom you may have caused to sin.

Eternal rest grant unto them, O Lord, and let perpetual light shine upon them. May they rest in peace. Amen.

Prayers of Release

*"Truly, I say to you, whatever you bind on earth shall
be bound in heaven, and whatever you loose on earth
shall be loosed in heaven." — Matthew 18:18*

"Some souls would suffer in purgatory until the day of judgment if they
were not relieved by the prayers of the church" — St. Robert Bellarmine.

Reflection: "From the beginning the Church has honored the memory of the dead and offered prayers in suffrage for them, above all the Eucharistic sacrifice, so that, thus purified, they may attain the beatific vision of God" (*Catechism of the Catholic Church,* n. 1032*).* Many die unprepared. Without sufficient penance. Without the sacraments. No one to pray for them. Offer a Mass for the most abandoned souls. The Mass is the summit of our faith. It is the highest act of worship, the highest form of prayer.

---

*Eternal rest grant unto them, O Lord, and let perpetual
light shine upon them. May they rest in peace. Amen.*

God's Plan for You

For I know the plans I have for you, says the LORD, *plans for welfare and not for evil, to give you a future and a hope.* — *Jeremiah 29:11*

"Wouldn't it be terrible after the sufferings in this life, to still suffer in the next!

"To avoid purgatory is to magnify the redemption of Christ. Where sin abounds, grace super-abounds. We are given a superabundance of grace for the attainment of our salvation. We must strive to attain immediate entry into heaven because God desires it and it is part of His plan" — Father Martin Jugie, Assumptionist, Byzantine scholar, author.

Reflection: Implore God that you may avoid purgatory. Live the Commandments and stick to His plan.

Eternal rest grant unto them, O Lord, and let perpetual light shine upon them. May they rest in peace. Amen.

Go Straight to Heaven

In all you do, remember the end of your life,
and then you will never sin. — Sirach 7:36

"The large number of souls who suffer in purgatory and for whom the Church prays daily did not need to go there. If we think in human terms, God does not wish for us to need purgatory. God does not put us here on earth, where we are tested and are suffering after the fall, only to let us suffer again — and much worse — in purgatory. Everyone receives enough graces in order to go straight to God after passing the trials on earth. Purgatory is an emergency entry to heaven for those who have wasted their time. However, what God considered the exception became the rule, and the rule — to go straight to heaven — became the exception" — Dr. Hubert van Dijk, O.R.C., German priest who translated this teaching of St. Thérèse of Lisieux on purgatory, author.

Reflection: The *Catechism of the Catholic Church* says that "grace is *favor,* the *free and underserved help* that God gives us to respond to his call to become children of God, adoptive sons, partakers of the divine nature and of eternal life" (n. 1996). However, it is up to us to acknowledge and accept it.

Eternal rest grant unto them, O Lord, and let perpetual
light shine upon them. May they rest in peace. Amen.

Free Us!

*When shall I come and behold the face of God? My tears
have been my food day and night. — Psalm 42:3*

The story is told of two Dominican priests in a religious community who
had differing opinions on whether it was better to say Mass for the living
or for the dead. The first argued: "The souls in purgatory are sure of their
salvation, while sinners on earth are exposed to the danger of falling into
hell." The second nodded but pointed out: "Suppose you met two beggars,
the one was sick, maimed, and helpless, absolutely incapable of earning
his livelihood; the other, on the contrary, although in great distress, was
young and vigorous. Which of the two would deserve the greater share of
your alms?" The answer was obvious: the one who was unable to work.

Then the second priest continued: "That's just the case with regard to
sinners on earth and holy souls in purgatory. The souls can no longer help
themselves. The time of prayer, confession, and good works is past for
them. We alone are able to relieve them."

He concluded: "Let's be compassionate to sinners but not forget they
have all the means of salvation at their disposal. They must break the
bonds of sin. Doesn't it seem evident that the suffering souls are in greater
need and so merit a larger share in our charity?"

The first had to agree that it did.

Reflection: Entrust your most special needs to the most abandoned
souls in purgatory. They are very powerful.

---

*Eternal rest grant unto them, O Lord, and let perpetual
light shine upon them. May they rest in peace. Amen.*

Sparks Flying

*In the time of their visitation they will shine forth, and
will run like sparks through the stubble.* — *Wisdom 3:7*

A holy religious, John of Alvernia, saw the consoling effects of offering
the sacrifice of the Mass on All Souls' Day. He saw purgatory opened and
many souls coming forward who were delivered by the sacrifice of propitiation (the Mass). They resembled numerous sparks that escaped from a
burning furnace.

Reflection: Envision the eternal joy you are giving to the most grateful souls.

---

*Eternal rest grant unto them, O Lord, and let perpetual
light shine upon them. May they rest in peace. Amen.*

The Blood of Christ Frees Souls

*I will lift up the cup of salvation and call
on the name of the LORD.* — Psalm 116:13

St. Mary Magdalen de Pazzi learned from Our Lord to offer the Blood of Jesus to the Eternal Father. It was a simple commemoration of the Passion. She did this at least fifty times a day. In one of her ecstasies she saw a large number of sinners converted and souls delivered from purgatory through this practice.

Reflection: Offer the most Precious Blood of Jesus to the Eternal Father, just as St. Mary Magdalen did. Pray: "Eternal Father, I offer Thee the Precious Blood of Jesus in satisfaction for my sins and for the needs of Holy Mother Church."

---

*Eternal rest grant unto them, O Lord, and let perpetual
light shine upon them. May they rest in peace. Amen.*

Purgatory Island

"Unless you repent you will all likewise perish." — *Luke 13:5*

An ancient pilgrimage place called St. Patrick's Purgatory is located on Station Island in Lough Derg, County Donegal, Ireland. St. Patrick stayed in a cave there, where he had visions of heaven, hell, and purgatory. For more than a thousand years pilgrims have come to this place, fasted for three days, and walked barefoot, doing a bit of "purgatory." It is a journey of conversion of the heart. It is a place rich in faith, and the pilgrims offer sacrifice and prayers for the souls in purgatory.

Reflection: During the "Great Lent," some rites in the Eastern Church mark All Souls Saturdays, celebrating the Divine Liturgy for the souls of departed loved ones. Come closer to God and the holy souls this Lent by dedicating Saturday Mass and Holy Communion for your departed family and friends.

Eternal rest grant unto them, O Lord, and let perpetual light shine upon them. May they rest in peace. Amen.

Too Good for Hell

*"Many shall purify themselves, and make themselves
white, and be refined." — Daniel 12:10*

"There are so many men who are not sufficiently guilty as to be closed in entirely upon themselves — which is Hell — not yet sufficiently ready for this marriage of eternal love — which is the Beatific Vision — there must be an intermediary stage — which is purgatory" — Father Maurice Zundel, Swiss mystic, philosopher, author.

Reflection: The holy souls will do their utmost to preserve us from the fires of hell. Pray for the souls who are in the deepest purgatory.

---

*Eternal rest grant unto them, O Lord, and let perpetual
light shine upon them. May they rest in peace. Amen.*

"Ite Ad Ioseph" — "Go to Joseph"

Whoever honors his father atones for sins, and whoever glorifies
his mother is like one who lays up treasure. — Sirach 3:3-4

"The Son of God, having the keys of Paradise, has given one to His Immaculate Mother and the other to St. Joseph. You who so much love your dearly departed, go to Joseph! He is the mediator of all who are detained in those cleansing fires, he exercises special influence on behalf of those who during life expressed great zeal and in honoring him" — Father Francis Xavier Lasance, priest, author.

Reflection: Pray for the dying. They become the holy souls. Say this prayer daily for the dying: "St. Joseph, foster father of Our Lord, Jesus Christ, true spouse of Mary, ever Virgin, pray for us and all those who will die this day or night. Amen." Join the Pious Union of St. Joseph for the dying. (See page 395 for information on Pious Union Membership.)

Eternal rest grant unto them, O Lord, and let perpetual
light shine upon them. May they rest in peace. Amen.

MARCH 20

A Consoling Doctrine

"Do not be afraid." — *Matthew 28:10*

"The thought of purgatory is productive rather of consolation than of terror.... Great as the torments of purgatory are ... the interior consolations granted there are nevertheless so ineffable that no earthly bliss and enjoyment can equal them" — St. Francis de Sales.

Reflection: Be not afraid of purgatory! It is not a punishment. It is a *loving* purgatory. It is God's love that heals the heart, purifies, and matures the holy souls. It is God's love at work in us urging us to help their condition of existence. It is God's love purifying us for eternal life. It is a masterpiece of God's infinite love and mercy.

Eternal rest grant unto them, O Lord, and let perpetual light shine upon them. May they rest in peace. Amen.

Angels' Comfort

Bless the LORD, all his hosts, his ministers
that do his will! — Psalm 103:21

"St. Margaret of Cortona was praying to Our Lord with tears for all the friends she had lost; they had appeared to her in such a lamentable condition that she could not endure the sight. Our Savior said to her: 'The pains they endure are very great, but would be incomparably greater if they were not visited and consoled by My angels, the sight of whom comforts them in their sufferings and refreshes them in the heat'" — Father Jean Bolland, S.J., Flemish scholar.

Reflection: The guardian angels assist with a special zeal those souls in purgatory who have been most devoted to them during life. Be an Angel of Mercy — console the blessed souls. They, in turn, will console you.

Eternal rest grant unto them, O Lord, and let perpetual
light shine upon them. May they rest in peace. Amen.

No Rebellion in Purgatory

Righteous art thou, O LORD, and right
are thy judgments. — Psalm 119:137

"The souls in purgatory, having their wills perfectly conformed to the will of God, and partaking of His goodness, remain satisfied with their condition. I see that the Being of God is so pure, far more than one can imagine, that should a soul see in itself the least mote of imperfection, it would rather cast itself into a thousand hells than go with that spot into the presence of the Divine Majesty" — St. Catherine of Genoa.

Reflection: Are you willing to offer your sufferings for the imprisoned souls?

Eternal rest grant unto them, O Lord, and let perpetual
light shine upon them. May they rest in peace. Amen.

Bring Me Souls

*"This is my blood of the covenant, which is
poured out for many." — Mark 14:24*

"Today bring to Me the souls who are in the prison of Purgatory, and immerse them in the abyss of My mercy. Let the torrents of My Blood cool down their scorching flames. All these souls are greatly loved by Me. They are making retribution to My justice. It is in your power to bring them relief. Draw all the indulgences from the treasury of My Church and offer them on their behalf. Oh, if you only knew the torments they suffer, you would continually offer for them the alms of the spirit and pay off their debt to My justice" — St. Faustina (*Diary*, 1226).

Reflection: Resolve to gain indulgences daily for your deceased family and friends. (See page 395 for the definition of "indulgence.")

*Eternal rest grant unto them, O Lord, and let perpetual
light shine upon them. May they rest in peace. Amen.*

Looking Out for You

Now that you have been set free from sin and
have become slaves of God, the reward you get is
sanctification and its end, eternal life. — *Romans 6:22*

"If I could know for certain that I had the happiness of releasing one of those souls, all my dread and fear of eternity would vanish; I should regard my salvation as assured. For such a soul could not witness me going to perdition without imploring mercy for me so fervently that the Lord would grant me His mercy" — Bishop Joseph Colmar of Mainz, Germany.

Reflection: Imagine the number of souls you are releasing from purgatory today.

Eternal rest grant unto them, O Lord, and let perpetual
light shine upon them. May they rest in peace. Amen.

Perpetual Intercessor

"My soul magnifies the Lord, and my spirit rejoices in God my Savior, for he has regarded the low estate of his handmaiden. For behold, henceforth all generations will call me blessed." — Luke 1:48

"O how amiable and benevolent Mary shows herself to them that suffer in purgatory; for through her they continually receive comfort and consolation" — St. Vincent Ferrer.

Reflection: "Behold, I am the handmaid of the Lord; let it be done to me according to your word" (Lk 1:38). The whole world awaited Mary's reply. Mary said, "Yes." What is your reply? Pray for the souls most devoted to our Blessed Mother. Wrap these precious souls in Our Lady's mantle with your prayers. Pray the Angelus (page 390).

Eternal rest grant unto them, O Lord, and let perpetual light shine upon them. May they rest in peace. Amen.

Now Is the Time

*"At the acceptable time I have listened to you, and helped you
on the day of salvation." Behold, now is the acceptable time;
behold, now is the day of salvation. — 2 Corinthians 6:2-3*

"If we ever entertained for some of those hapless Prisoners of the King
sentiments of tender affection, of engrossing love; if ever we rejoiced in
their presence and experienced the bliss of their unfailing sympathy; if
ever we vowed undying remembrance of their manifold kindnesses, and
proffered them the tribute of our enduring gratitude — now is the time
to make our protestations, now the time to prove the genuineness of our
love" — Reverend A. B. O'Neill, C.S.C., author.

Reflection: We must help the suffering souls reach the object of
their love. Never lose the sense of urgency to assist the souls.

*Eternal rest grant unto them, O Lord, and let perpetual
light shine upon them. May they rest in peace. Amen.*

Eternal Light

*"And you shall command the people of Israel that they
bring to you pure beaten olive oil for the light, that a lamp
be set up to burn continually." — Exodus 27:20*

On the Day of Atonement (Yom Kippur), Jews read the Old Testament Scriptures (Torah), and pray for those who have died (*Yizkor*). Just as Jews light candles in memory of the dead, so, too, Catholics light votive candles.

For Catholics, the burning lamp or candle signifies Christ, the eternal Light, Whom we implore in our prayers to shine upon the departed. At the same time they are also a continual admonition for the living to remember their deceased brethren; they are alms for the suffering souls, symbolizing charity; for as the flame gradually consumes the blessed candle, thus charity reduces the torments of the purifying fire.

At *Yizkor*, Jews traditionally wear white burial shrouds as they pray for their beloved dead. This brings to mind for us how Our Lord was wrapped in His burial shroud before being placed in the tomb of Joseph of Arimathea.

Reflection: Light a blessed candle in honor of all souls. St. Athanasius tells us "this is pleasing to God and merits great reward."

---

*Eternal rest grant unto them, O Lord, and let perpetual
light shine upon them. May they rest in peace. Amen.*

The Present Moment

*You may have to suffer various trials, that the genuineness
of your faith, more precious than gold which though
perishable is tested by fire, may redound to praise and glory
and honor at the revelation of Jesus Christ. — 1 Peter 1:6-7*

St. Gemma Galgani always had some particular soul on her mind for whose relief she was especially interested. "Yes, suffer!" she would say. "Suffer for sinners, and even more the suffering souls."

Reflection: "Oh, if only the suffering soul knew how it is loved by God, it would die of joy and excess of happiness! Some day, we will know the value of suffering, but then we will no longer be able to suffer. The present moment is ours" — St. Faustina (*Diary*, 963).

---

*Eternal rest grant unto them, O Lord, and let perpetual
light shine upon them. May they rest in peace. Amen.*

Tears and Sighs

The Lord shall have washed away the filth of the daughters of Zion and cleansed the bloodstains of Jerusalem from its midst by a spirit of judgment and by a spirit of burning. — Isaiah 4:47

St. Teresa of Ávila in her spiritual masterpiece, *The Interior Castle*, speaks about the level of prayer where the soul's growing desire for God is similar to the longing for God of the souls in purgatory. She says that the soul's yearning for God reveals itself in tears and sighs and unquenchable thirst. This comes from the soul's deep burning love for God. It is like a smoldering fire, the heat of which is quite unbearable. At times the soul feels as though it was wounded with an arrow of fire. God purifies the soul in order for it to enter the "seventh mansion" (the image St. Teresa uses to mean the level of prayer to enter the abode of God). It is much like the souls being purified before they can see God.

Reflection: Let us help the holy souls who are richest in merits in God's sight. Quench their thirst, dry their tears with a Holy Mass.

Eternal rest grant unto them, O Lord, and let perpetual light shine upon them. May they rest in peace. Amen.

Making Amends

"Break off your sins by practicing righteousness, and your iniquities by showing mercy to the oppressed." — Daniel 4:27

"Absolution takes away sin, but it does not remedy all the disorders sin has caused.

"Raised up from sin, the sinner must still recover his full spiritual health by doing something more to make amends for the sin he must 'make satisfaction for' or 'expiate' his sin. This satisfaction is called 'penance.' ... It can consist of prayer, an offering, works of mercy, service of neighbor, voluntary self-denial, sacrifices, and above all the patient acceptance of the cross we must bear" — *Catechism of the Catholic Church* (nn. 1459-1460).

Reflection: Be aware of even the smallest sin.

Eternal rest grant unto them, O Lord, and let perpetual light shine upon them. May they rest in peace. Amen.

Our Souls Demand Purgatory

*For we must all appear before the judgment seat of Christ, so
that each one may receive recompense, according to what he
did in the body, whether good or evil. — 2 Corinthians 5:10*

"Of course I pray for the dead. At our age many of those we love are
dead. What sort of intercourse with God could I have if what I love best
were unmentionable to Him? I believe in purgatory. Our souls demand
purgatory, don't they? My favorite image on this matter comes from the
dentist's chair. I hope that when the tooth of life is drawn, and I am 'coming round' a voice will say, 'Rinse your mouth out with this.' This will be
purgatory. The rinsing may take longer than I can now imagine. The taste
of this may be more fiery and astringent than my present sensibility could
endure. But ... it will [not] be disgusting and unhallowed" — C. S. Lewis,
lay theologian, Christian apologist, poet, author.

Reflection: Be charitable in your speech.

---

*Eternal rest grant unto them, O Lord, and let perpetual
light shine upon them. May they rest in peace. Amen.*

Faithful Friends

*A faithful friend is a sturdy shelter: he that has
found one has found a treasure.* — Sirach 6:14

"The holy souls in purgatory. Out of charity, out of justice, and out of excusable selfishness — they have such power with God! — remember them often in your sacrifices and in your prayers. May you be able to say when you speak of them, 'My good friends the souls in purgatory'" — St. Josemaría Escrivá.

Reflection: Offer a Spiritual Communion for the departed souls (see page 394). A Spiritual Communion reminds you of the indwelling of the Most Holy Trinity within you, but also increases the indwelling by a new inpouring of the Precious Blood into your soul.

---

*Eternal rest grant unto them, O Lord, and let perpetual
light shine upon them. May they rest in peace. Amen.*

APRIL 2

Three States

*I press on toward the goal for the prize of the upward
call of God in Christ Jesus. — Philippians 3:14*

"Three possible states await a soul after death: a state of perfect Love without suffering which is heaven; a state of suffering without Love which is Hell, and a state of Love with suffering which is Purgatory. Purgatory is the creation of the Mercy of God" — Venerable Archbishop Fulton J. Sheen.

Reflection: Venerable Archbishop Sheen shares: "The human heart is not shaped like a valentine heart, perfect and regular in contour; it is slightly irregular in shape, as if a small piece of it were missing out of its side. The missing part may very well symbolize a piece that a spear tore out of the universal heart of humanity on the Cross, but it probably symbolizes something more. It may very well mean that when God created each human heart, he kept a small sample of it in heaven, and sent the rest of it into the world, where it would each day learn the lesson that it could never be really happy, that it could never be really wholly in love, that it could never be really wholehearted until it rested with the Risen Christ in an eternal Easter." Invoke God's mercy for those who will die alone.

---

*Eternal rest grant unto them, O Lord, and let perpetual
light shine upon them. May they rest in peace. Amen.*

APRIL 3

Spiritual Parents

Do good to a godly man and you will be repaid — if not by him, certainly by the Most High. — Sirach 12:2

"If by your prayers, sufferings, or other good works, you have obtained a good death for the dying sinner, you should look upon yourself as a mother to that soul. You have placed it in purgatory. Now you will assist, by all the means you can, in obtaining its release from that place of imprisonment. To do this, you should be very anxious to obtain indulgences. St. Leonard thought so highly of this practice [of obtaining indulgences] that he considered a person on the road to sanctity [anyone] who adopted it" — Mother Mary Potter, foundress of the Little Company of Mary Sisters, author.

Reflection: Pick out your favorite indulgenced prayers to pray daily and apply them to those who will die a sudden death. (In "Prayers Recommened in Reflections" — starting on page 390 — the indulgenced prayers are: Act of Contrition; The Angelus; Chaplet of Divine Mercy; Guardian Angel Prayer; Hail, Holy Queen; *Memorare*; Morning Offering; Psalm 130 ["*De Profundis*"]; *Te Deum*; and Spiritual Communion.)

Eternal rest grant unto them, O Lord, and let perpetual light shine upon them. May they rest in peace. Amen.

Eternal Remembrance

*In the days of his flesh, Jesus offered up prayers and
supplications, with loud cries and tears. — Hebrews 5:7*

"As long as my heart shall beat in my breast, as long as I can raise my eyes and hands towards heaven, I will not cease to pray for their souls" — St. Ambrose on praying for his brother, Satyrus, and friends.

Reflection: Pray for your deceased relatives, each one by name.

---

*Eternal rest grant unto them, O Lord, and let perpetual
light shine upon them. May they rest in peace. Amen.*

The Mystical Body Unites

Whether we live or whether we die, we are the Lord's. — Romans 14:8

"We believe in the communion of all the faithful of Christ, those who are pilgrims on earth, the dead who are being purified, and the blessed in heaven, all together forming one Church; and we believe that in this communion, the merciful love of God and his saints is always [attentive] to our prayers" — *Catechism of the Catholic Church* (n. 962).

Reflection: The saints pray to God to inspire the living to offer their good works for the dead; they pray to God to apply the superabundance of their merits to the holy souls; the saints beseech Our Lady and even Christ Himself, who has an infinite treasure of satisfactions to apply to the holy souls. Invoke the powerful intercession of the family of saints, who look with compassion on the holy souls.

Eternal rest grant unto them, O Lord, and let perpetual light shine upon them. May they rest in peace. Amen.

Good Grieving

*Water extinguishes a blazing fire: so
almsgiving atones for sin.* — Sirach 3:30

St. Jerome writes to the widower Pammachius: "Other husbands strew violets, lilies, and purple flowers on the tombs of their wives; our Pammachius waters the holy ashes and venerated bones with the balm of alms.... [K]now that water extinguishes fire, so does alms sin."

Reflection: Give alms to the poor, sick, and marginalized for the sake of these great lovers of God. Pope Benedict XVI said in his Lenten message for 2008 that sinners can often "feel far from God, fearful and almost incapable of turning to Him. By drawing close to others through almsgiving, we draw close to God; it can become an instrument for authentic conversion and reconciliation with Him and our brothers."

---

*Eternal rest grant unto them, O Lord, and let perpetual
light shine upon them. May they rest in peace. Amen.*

Always and Everywhere Give Thanks

"It is good to praise God and to exalt his name, worthily declaring the works of God. Do not be slow to give him thanks." — Tobit 12:6

"If we neither return thanks to God in tribulation, nor redeem sin with good works, we shall stay in the fire of purgatory until the above small sins be consumed like wood, hay and stubble.... But someone may say: 'I don't mind how long I stay there if at length I arrive at eternal life.' Let no one say this, dearest brethren, because that pain shall be severer than any punishment that can be either thought of or seen, or felt in this world. How can anyone know whether he is about to be purified through purgatory for days and months, or perhaps even for years?" — St. Caesarius of Arles.

Reflection: Identify some recurrent sin in your life needing to be eradicated.

Eternal rest grant unto them, O Lord, and let perpetual light shine upon them. May they rest in peace. Amen.

Mercy on Yourself

"Blessed are the merciful, for they shall obtain mercy."
— Matthew 5:7

As St. John of God wandered through the streets of Granada collecting alms for a hospital he intended to build, he called out: "Give alms, my brethren, for the love and pity of yourselves!"

Reflection: Are we as generous to others as God is to us? Give your time, talent, and treasures. Better to wear out than rust out. As Blessed Mother Teresa of Calcutta says: "Give until it hurts!" You are giving to Jesus in the poor.

Eternal rest grant unto them, O Lord, and let perpetual light shine upon them. May they rest in peace. Amen.

Greater Expectations

"Every one to whom much is given, of him
will much be required." — Luke 12:48

"The souls consecrated to God will have a special and more intense purgatory. And this is just, they receive more benefits. From those souls, on whom God has bestowed great and special graces, He demands a more faithful cooperation. Where grace has been augmented, there also the account has been increased" — Blessed James Alberione, Italian priest, founder of the Daughters of St. Paul and the Society of St. Paul, author.

Reflection: The most abandoned souls are clergy and consecrated religious. Recite seven Our Fathers, Hail Marys, and Glory Be's to obtain their pardon.

Eternal rest grant unto them, O Lord, and let perpetual
light shine upon them. May they rest in peace. Amen.

APRIL 10

Suffering

The crucible is for silver, and the furnace is for gold,
and the Lord tries hearts. — Proverbs 17:3

"You ask me what these souls suffer; the answer would be easier if you had asked me what they do *not* suffer" — Father Louis Bourdaloue, S.J., French preacher.

Reflection: Even the smallest suffering offered in love is priceless in God's sight. When we suffer for the holy souls it becomes a gift of inestimable value. Servant of God, Father John Hardon, S.J., shares: "Love *wants* to suffer for the Beloved.... Love wants to expiate the sins that have so deeply penetrated mankind. Love wants to make up for the lack of love among those who sin. Love wants to relieve the debt of suffering that sinners owe to God. Love wants to give God what sinners are depriving Him of by their sins."

Eternal rest grant unto them, O Lord, and let perpetual
light shine upon them. May they rest in peace. Amen.

Sacrifice of Love

*Do not neglect to do good and to share what you have, for
such sacrifices are pleasing to God. — Hebrews 13:16*

"St. Gemma Galgani offered herself as a victim for the conversion of sinners but she did not forget the souls in purgatory. She offered herself as
a victim for them, too. 'My Guardian Angel told me that Jesus would
send me some special suffering, which would last two hours.' She gives an
account of these two hours. 'I had a frightful headache, and every movement caused me intense suffering.' Heaven accepted these generous expia-
tions of this heroic soul, and the souls in purgatory found their sufferings
lightened and the time of their captivity shortened" — Father Martin
Jugie, Assumptionist, Byzantine scholar, author.

Reflection: If you experience a headache, remember, heaven is waiting to accept your sufferings for the relief of the suffering servants.

---

*Eternal rest grant unto them, O Lord, and let perpetual
light shine upon them. May they rest in peace. Amen.*

In Silent Resignation

God's grace and mercy are with his elect, and he
watches over his holy ones. — Wisdom 4:15

"St. John once had a wonderful vision. He saw a temple, and, in the sanctuary of this temple, perceived an altar, and beneath this altar, the multitude of suffering souls.

"These souls are not in *front of the altar*, as one commentator remarks; they are not permitted to be there. They participate in the fruit of the Eucharistic Sacrifice only indirectly, by means of intercession. They are *below the altar*, and await, resigned, although in torment, the portion we are willing to convey to their lips" — Father Charles Arminjon, French preacher, author.

Reflection: Make brief acts of Spiritual Communions on behalf of the holy heroes by praying with St. Francis of Assisi: "May the burning and most sweet power of your love, O Lord Jesus Christ, I beseech you, absorb my mind, that I may die through love of your love, who was graciously pleased to die through love of my love. Amen."

Eternal rest grant unto them, O Lord, and let perpetual
light shine upon them. May they rest in peace. Amen.

A Life Forever Changed

*Stretch forth your hand to the poor, so that your
blessing may be complete.* — *Sirach 7:32*

St. Peter Damian lost his parents when he was a boy. He was raised by a brother who treated him with cruelty. One day St. Peter found a large coin. He thought of the many things he could purchase with the money. However, he thought of those poorer than himself, so he gave the money to a priest to offer a Mass for the holy souls. From that day on his life was forever changed. Another brother who was kind and gentle took care of him, and allowed him to study to become a priest.

Reflection: Pray for the soul of the priest who baptized you. It is not necessary to remember his name. The good God knows who he is!

---

*Eternal rest grant unto them, O Lord, and let perpetual
light shine upon them. May they rest in peace. Amen.*

APRIL 14

Stairway to Heaven

"Truly, truly, I say to you, you will see heaven opened, and the angels of God ascending and descending upon the Son of man." — John 1:51

Outside of Rome is a church called Santa Maria Scala Coeli. St. Bernard lived nearby in the Monastery of Saints Vincent and Anastasius. One day during the celebration of Holy Mass, St. Bernard saw an unending stairway that led up to heaven. By means of the stairway many angels ascended and descended, carrying from purgatory to paradise souls freed by the Sacrifice of Jesus — a sacrifice renewed by priests on altars all over the world. This vision is captured in a painting above the altar where St. Bernard offered Masses for the souls in purgatory at that church.

Reflection: The Holy Sacrifice of the Mass is the "stairway to heaven" for the holy souls. Strive to go deep into the Mass.

Eternal rest grant unto them, O Lord, and let perpetual light shine upon them. May they rest in peace. Amen.

APScriptRIL 15

Grazie, Padre Pio

For what thanksgiving can we render to God for you, for all the joy which we feel for your sake before our God? — 1 Thessalonians 3:9

"I was talking with some souls while on their way from purgatory to heaven, stopped here to thank me because I remembered them in my Mass this morning.... [M]ore souls of the dead, than of the living, climb this mountain to attend my Masses seek my prayers" — St. Pio of Pietrelcina.

Reflection: The next time you attend Mass, especially include the holy souls during the Eucharistic Prayer.

Eternal rest grant unto them, O Lord, and let perpetual light shine upon them. May they rest in peace. Amen.

Purgatorial Truth

I delight to do thy will, O my God. — *Psalm 40:8*

"It is a two-edged sword. However, no earthy happiness can equal their joy. For these [holy] souls:

"Are in continual union with God. They are in perfect resignation to God's holy will. They will only what He wills. If the gates of heaven were opened to them, if they still have any stain of sin in themselves, they would not attempt to appear before God. They purify themselves voluntarily in love only to please God. They are impeccable. They have not the slightest impatience and do not commit the smallest fault. They love God above all things with a perfect, pure, and unselfish love. They are comforted by the angels. They are certain of their salvation. Their bitterness is wrapped in peace" — St. Francis de Sales.

Reflection: When praying the Lord's Prayer, recall, "Thy will be done!"

---

*Eternal rest grant unto them, O Lord, and let perpetual
light shine upon them. May they rest in peace. Amen.*

Happy Spring

"Blessed are those who have not seen and yet believe." — John 20:29

"'I'm making you a surprise,' he called out. That was Dad, always thoughtful. By the following spring, as the surprise emerged, I had almost forgotten. 'Crocuses!' exclaimed one of the kids. Not in a border, but popping up all across the lawn. Pink, blue, even purple, their little blossoms sweeping across the drab landscape. 'I planted the bulbs so you can see them from the window,' Dad explained. 'Spring will come faster that way.' How right he was. But Dad's enjoyment of his unique garden was brief. A few years later, he slipped away and the remaining crocuses followed his lead. Where are you, Dad? Can we count on the fact that our loved ones are with us all the time? How I wanted to believe. Around the corner, I saw one crocus in my favorite color, pink, waving at me in the wind. The crocus bloomed for one day. My Father's Birthday" — Joan Wester Anderson, author.

Reflection: Contribute flowers to the church altar to represent a true garden of life for those loved ones who are no longer with you in body.

Eternal rest grant unto them, O Lord, and let perpetual light shine upon them. May they rest in peace. Amen.

APRIL 18

An Exchange of Prayers

But you are a chosen race, a royal priesthood,
a holy nation, God's own people. — 1 Peter 2:9

"You the living can do everything for us, and we can do everything for you. It is an exchange of prayers" — The soul of a deceased priest.

Reflection: Many priests have no family to pray for them. Pray for our deceased shepherds in a special way. They will be with you at the hour of your death. Invoke Jesus, the Eternal High Priest, to lead all souls of priests into heaven. Offer Masses for their souls.

Eternal rest grant unto them, O Lord, and let perpetual
light shine upon them. May they rest in peace. Amen.

Burning Longings

*O God, thou art my God, I seek thee, my soul
thirsts for thee; my flesh faints for thee, as in a dry
and weary land where no water is. — Psalm 63:1*

"By death the soul is freed from the miseries of the body; the intellect becomes brighter; the soul realizes to a great extent the infinite beauties and glories of God; and with ardent desires, and burning longings, seeks and sighs to possess her God" — St. Thomas Aquinas (Homily 48).

Reflection: Implore the purifying love of God to prepare the hearts, minds, and souls of all the faithful departed.

---

*Eternal rest grant unto them, O Lord, and let perpetual
light shine upon them. May they rest in peace. Amen.*

First Act

I thank my God in all my remembrance of you, always in every prayer of mine for you all making my prayer with joy, thankful for your partnership in the gospel from the first day until now. — Philippians 1:3-5

"There is no doubt that on their entrance into eternal glory the first favors which they ask of the Divine Mercy are for those who have opened to them the gates of Paradise, and they will never fail to pray for their benefactors, whenever they see them in any necessity or danger. In reverses of fortune, sicknesses, and accidents of all kinds they will be their protectors. Their zeal will increase when the interests of the soul are at stake; they will powerfully assist them to vanquish temptation, to practice good works, to die a Christian death, and to escape the sufferings of the other life" — Father Paolo Rossignoli, missionary, author.

Reflection: The holy souls pray incessantly for those who help them. Our prayer may be the key needed to open the gates of heaven for them.

Eternal rest grant unto them, O Lord, and let perpetual light shine upon them. May they rest in peace. Amen.

APRIL 21

Idle Talk

*O LORD, open thou my lips, and my mouth
shall show forth thy praise. — Psalm 51:15*

"I sometimes talk too much. A thing could be settled in one or two words, and as for me, I take too much time about it. But Jesus wants me to use that time to say some short indulgenced prayers for the souls in purgatory. And the Lord says that every word will be weighed on the day of judgment" — St. Faustina (*Diary*, 274).

Reflection: Cultivate interior recollection through silence in order to hear the voice of God. Then we can say with Samuel: "Speak, O Lord, for your servant is listening."

---

*Eternal rest grant unto them, O Lord, and let perpetual
light shine upon them. May they rest in peace. Amen.*

Indulgence without Conditions

"In all things I have shown you that by so toiling one must help the weak, remembering the words of the Lord Jesus, how he said, 'It is more blessed to give than to receive.'" — Acts 20:35

"The chief indulgence, which is in reach of everybody, and can be gained without the ordinary conditions, is that of charity which 'covers a multitude of sins'" — St. Thérèse of Lisieux.

Reflection: Pray for all the souls who have died without the benefit of the sacraments of the Church.

Eternal rest grant unto them, O Lord, and let perpetual light shine upon them. May they rest in peace. Amen.

The Saving Host

*"They have washed their robes and made them white
in the blood of the Lamb." — Revelation 7:14*

When St. John of Ávila was on his deathbed, his confreres asked him what he desired most after his death. The saint promptly answered, "Masses ... Masses ... nothing else but Masses!"

Reflection: St. Alphonsus says: "Just as all creation, the heavens and the earth, the sun, the moon and the stars, the mountains and oceans, all men and angels are nothing in comparison with God, so no good works, however holy, are equal to one Mass. The Mass is God Himself." Enroll your deceased loved ones in one of the Perpetual Mass Remembrances (see page 395 for more information).

---

*Eternal rest grant unto them, O Lord, and let perpetual
light shine upon them. May they rest in peace. Amen.*

A Swap

The offering of a righteous man anoints the altar, and its pleasing odor rises before the Most High. The sacrifice of a righteous man is acceptable, and the memory of it will not be forgotten. — Sirach 35:6-7

During a sermon one day, St. John Vianney gave the example of a priest who, celebrating Mass for a deceased friend, after the Consecration prayed as follows: "Holy and Eternal Father, let us make an exchange. You possess the soul of my friend in purgatory; I have the Body of Your Son in my hands. You liberate my friend for me, and I offer to You Your Son, with all the merits of His Passion and Death."

Reflection: Here is an offer you cannot refuse: Pray for the holy souls in exchange for their prayers. The more you pray for them, the more powerful their intercession will be for you!

Eternal rest grant unto them, O Lord, and let perpetual light shine upon them. May they rest in peace. Amen.

APRIL 25

In Union with His Most Precious Blood

*"This cup which is poured out for you is the
new covenant in my blood." — Luke 22:20*

St. Bernadette was so full of compassion for the souls in purgatory that she
would often say to her religious sisters: "I have heard Mass for the souls in
purgatory: nothing but the Precious Blood of Jesus applied for them can
liberate them."

Reflection: Pray with St. Bernadette: "Precious Blood of Jesus, cover
all souls with your merciful love!"

---

*Eternal rest grant unto them, O Lord, and let perpetual
light shine upon them. May they rest in peace. Amen.*

Bonds of Fidelity and Gratitude

To all God's beloved ... who are called to be saints: Grace to you and peace from God our Father and the Lord Jesus Christ. — Romans 1:7

"The memory of those who have gone before us, to whom we are linked by bonds of fidelity and gratitude, must also accompany us in all the acts of our daily life. For this is the memorial they deserve; this redounds to their honor; this is the spirit of Christian prayer for the dead, which is inseparable from Christian life and practice" — St. John XXIII.

Reflection: St. Cyprian wrote: "All our friends who have arrived wait for us. They desire vividly that we participate in their own beatitude, and are full of solicitude in our regard." Prayer is the inseparable link in the chain of grace for the holy souls. Be saturated with prayer. Pray longer than usual, recalling those you were linked with in this life.

Eternal rest grant unto them, O Lord, and let perpetual light shine upon them. May they rest in peace. Amen.

APRIL 27

Supernatural Charity

Who is he? And we will call him blessed, for he has done wonderful things among his people. Who has been tested by it and been found perfect? Let it be for him a ground for boasting. Who has had the power to transgress and did not transgress, and to do evil and did not do it? His prosperity will be established, and the assembly will relate his acts of charity. — Sirach 31:9-11

St. John Paul II reinvigorated the connection between the Church Militant on earth and the Church Suffering in purgatory. He stated that giving the holy souls your indulgence is the "highest act of supernatural charity" (Bull of Indiction for the Jubilee Year 2000).

Reflection: Charity begins at home. Offer Masses for your ancestors. On Divine Mercy Sunday offer your indulgence for the holy souls in purgatory.

Eternal rest grant unto them, O Lord, and let perpetual light shine upon them. May they rest in peace. Amen.

Pangs of Purgatory Lead to Ineffable Bliss

This is evidence of the righteous judgment of God, that
you may be made worthy of the kingdom of God, for
which you are suffering. — 2 Thessalonians 1:5

St. Mary Magdalen de Pazzi saw the soul of her brother in purgatory. Even though he led a good life, certain faults had not been sufficiently expiated in life. Struck with this vision, she went to her superior and said: "O my dear Mother, how terrible are the pangs of purgatory! Never could I have believed it, had not God manifested it to me ... and, nevertheless, I cannot call them cruel; rather are they advantageous, since they lead to the ineffable bliss of Paradise."

Reflection: Remember that in purgatory: "No pain, no gain!"

Eternal rest grant unto them, O Lord, and let perpetual
light shine upon them. May they rest in peace. Amen.

Offer Three Prayers

"The LORD bless you and keep you: The LORD make his face to shine upon you, and be gracious to you: The LORD lift up his countenance upon you, and give you peace." — Numbers 6:24-26

"On April 29, 1926, the soul of Sister Henry, who had recently died, asked St. Faustina to offer one Mass and three ejaculatory prayers [Eternal Rest Prayer] for her. And when that was done, Sister Henry's soul returned and said with gratitude, 'May God repay you' " — St. Faustina (*Diary*, 21).

Reflection: Pray the Eternal Rest Prayer (see below) three times.

Eternal rest grant unto them, O Lord, and let perpetual light shine upon them. May they rest in peace. Amen.

A Useless Leaf Hinders Christ's Grace

"I am the vine, you are the branches. He who abides
in me, and I in him, he it is that bears much fruit, for
apart from me you can do nothing." — John 15:5

"And if you turn to purgatory, there you will find my gentle immeasurable providence toward those poor souls who foolishly wasted their time. Now, because they are separated from their bodies, they no longer have time in which to merit. Therefore, I have provided that you who are still in mortal life should have time for them. I mean that by giving alms and having my ministers say the Divine Office, by fasting and praying while you are in the state of grace, you can by my mercy shorten their time of purification. O tender providence!

"I have told you all this about the soul's interior life and your salvation to make you fall in love with my providence and clothe yourself in the light of faith and firm hope. Thus you will free yourself of selfishness and, in all that is yours to do, trust in me without any slavish fear" — Jesus to St. Catherine of Siena.

Reflection: Look into your heart. What hay, wood, or stubble have you built upon the foundation of grace Christ laid in your life? How many useless leaves hinder the branches of your vineyard and damage the promise of its fruit?

Eternal rest grant unto them, O Lord, and let perpetual
light shine upon them. May they rest in peace. Amen.

The Choicest of Mary's Children

*Do not forsake her, and she will keep you; love her and she
will guard you. She will place on your head a fair garland; she
will bestow on you a beautiful crown. — Proverbs 4:6, 9*

"The lives of the saints, religious orders, confraternities are full of revelations and anecdotes which prove Our Lady is exercising her power in favor of the holy souls. Devotions practiced in her honor are most helpful in aiding the holy heroes. Masses in her honor, Masses offered for the souls most devout to her, alms, whether spiritual or material, works of mercy, reciting her rosary which is richly indulgenced, visiting her shrines, honoring her pictures, and statues, all used for the benefit of the holy souls" — Father H. J. Coleridge, S.J., preacher, author.

Reflection: Consecrate yourself to Our Lady: "O Holy Mary, my Mistress, into your blessed trust and special keeping, into the bosom of your tender mercy, I commend my soul and my body this day, every day of my life, and at the hour of my death. To you I entrust all my hope and consolations, all my trials and miseries, my life and the end of my life, that through your most holy intercession and your merits, all my actions may be ordered and disposed according to your will and that of your Divine Son. Amen."

---

*Eternal rest grant unto them, O Lord, and let perpetual
light shine upon them. May they rest in peace. Amen.*

Purify Yourself in His Love

*And I commanded the Levites that they should purify themselves
and come and guard the gates, to keep the Sabbath day holy.
Remember this also in my favor, O my God, and spare me according
to the greatness of thy steadfast love.* — *Nehemiah 13:22*

"Do not be afraid of going to purgatory because of its pain, but rather long not to go there because this pleases God who imposes this expiation so regretfully. From the moment you try to please Him in all things, if you have the unshakable confidence that He will purify you at every instant in His love and will leave in you no trace of sin, be very sure that you will not go to purgatory" — St. Thérèse of Lisieux.

Reflection: Our Lord to St. Faustina: "When you say this prayer with a contrite heart and with faith on behalf of some sinner, I will give them the grace of conversion. This is the prayer: 'O Blood and Water, which gushed forth from the Heart of Jesus, as a fount of Mercy for us, I trust in You!'" (*Diary*, 186-187).

---

*Eternal rest grant unto them, O Lord, and let perpetual
light shine upon them. May they rest in peace. Amen.*

Jesus' Merits

They are to do good, to be rich in good deeds,
liberal and generous. — 1 Timothy 6:18

"I was told that someone who had been our provincial was dead. I had some dealings with him and was indebted to him for some good deeds. He was a person of many virtues. As soon as I learned he was dead, I felt a lot of disturbance because I feared for his salvation in that he had been a superior for twenty years. Being a superior is something I am indeed very afraid of since I think having souls in one's charge involves a lot of danger; with much anxiety I went to an oratory. I offered up for him all the good I had done in my life, which must in fact amount to little, and so I asked the Lord to supply from His own merits what was necessary for that soul to be freed from purgatory. While beseeching the Lord for this as best I could, it seemed to me that person came out from the depths of the earth at my right side and that I saw him ascend to heaven with greatest happiness" — St. Teresa of Ávila.

Reflection: Be joyful! It will flow over to others. In gratitude for this intercession, offer to God on behalf of the blessed souls, the merits of all your joys this day.

Eternal rest grant unto them, O Lord, and let perpetual
light shine upon them. May they rest in peace. Amen.

Church Militant, Deliver Us!

*Therefore confess your sins to one another, and pray for
one another, that you may be healed. The prayer of a
righteous man has great power in its effects. — James 5:16*

"O Lord Jesus Christ, Just Judge, we implore you for the sake of your infinite mercy to turn away your eyes from our innumerable sins and to regard the merits of your passion and death. Imbue with your true love the religious, the priests and the faithful, so that they may hasten to our relief by their prayers, sacrifices, alms-deeds and indulgences. They can aid us if they wish; they can hasten our union with you, O God!" — St. Bridget, hearing these souls imploring Jesus for the intercession of priests and consecrated religious.

Reflection: Lord, bless our priests and religious who pray for the sinless souls in mercy, for "the merciful shall obtain mercy." Remember the priests and bishops who administered the sacraments to your family.

---

*Eternal rest grant unto them, O Lord, and let perpetual
light shine upon them. May they rest in peace. Amen.*

Mother of Mercy, Plead for Us!

At your right hand stands the queen in gold of Ophir. — Psalm 45:9

"Through her prayers and the application of her own merits, the Virgin has the power of freeing souls, especially her devotees, from purgatory" — St. Bernadine of Siena.

Reflection: "O most Holy Virgin, whose merits have raised you high above angel choirs by the very throne of the Eternal, hasten to help the holy souls!" Ask Our Lady to give you the graces you are not aware of and are in most need of. Beg Mary for the grace to contemplate Jesus through her eyes and her heart.

Recite the Hail, Holy Queen (see page 391).

---

*Eternal rest grant unto them, O Lord, and let perpetual
light shine upon them. May they rest in peace. Amen.*

All Torments on Earth

*For a day in thy courts is better than
a thousand elsewhere. — Psalm 84:10*

"It would be preferable to suffer all the possible torments of earth until Judgment Day than to pass one day in purgatory" — St. Cyril of Alexandria.

Reflection: The holy souls are concerned about their loved ones' salvation. They reach out to help those who are still on earth. Parents know the spiritual needs of their children, friends know how to support you on your journey, religious know the needs of their religious family. All these souls are moved by a tremendous resolve for us to become holy on earth and avoid the workshop of purgatory. Their prayers help us to recognize sin and understand its ugliness. The holy souls teach us that we must always strive for heaven. Today, work at developing a deeper appreciation for these great intercessors.

---

*Eternal rest grant unto them, O Lord, and let perpetual
light shine upon them. May they rest in peace. Amen.*

Joy in Prayer

Never flag in zeal, be aglow with the Spirit,
serve the Lord. — Romans 12:11

St. Gertrude never felt happier than on the days she prayed much for the relief of the souls in purgatory. She asked Jesus why she felt this way. He replied: "Because it would not be right for me to refuse the *fervent* prayers which you on these days pour out to me for the relief of my suffering spouses in purgatory, to refuse the prayers which you address to me on behalf of my captive spouses."

Reflection: Pray with fervor and zeal for the captive spouses. Include the souls of the whole world in your prayer.

Eternal rest grant unto them, O Lord, and let perpetual
light shine upon them. May they rest in peace. Amen.

MAY 8

Journey to God

*Therefore, my beloved, as you have always obeyed, so now not only
as in my presence but much more in my absence, work out your own
salvation with fear and trembling; for God is at work in you, both
to will and to work for his good pleasure.* — *Philippians 2:12*

Our life is a journey to God. Each person has a special vocation or calling
for the honor and glory of God. Theologians tell us there are three stages
or three main parts of our journey:

- The Purgative Way (conversion from sin to a state of grace)
- The Illuminative Way (mature faith)
- The Unitive Way (complete trust in God)

Purgatory is the fulfillment of life's goal when it is not completed on
earth.

Reflection: Strive to "work out your salvation with fear and trembling," to obtain perfect unity with God, offering your pain and
sufferings for the purgatorial souls. Remember, the value of your
offering is revealed in the depth of your charity.

---

*Eternal rest grant unto them, O Lord, and let perpetual
light shine upon them. May they rest in peace. Amen.*

Roses for the Holy Souls

*Let the favor of the LORD our God be upon us, and
establish thou the work of our hands upon us, yea, the
work of our hands establish thou it. — Psalm 90:17*

"Let us greatly value indulgences, since they have been bought with the Blood of our Savior. Let us not treat them with indifference, on the grounds that they are numerous and easy to gain. Let us choose our favorites among the indulgenced ejaculations, and often during the day let us drop them on purgatory like the petals of a refreshing rose. If ever we find ourselves in purgatory, we will know the value of that rose" — Father Martin Jugie, Assumptionist, Byzantine scholar, author.

Reflection: It is good to pray short indulgenced sighs of prayer during the day. It is a sigh of love understood by the God of Love. Pray these indulgenced prayers: "Heart of Jesus, burning with love of us, set our hearts on fire for love of You." "Immaculate Heart of Mary, pray for us." "Jesus, Mary, and Joseph I give you my heart and my soul!"

---

*Eternal rest grant unto them, O Lord, and let perpetual
light shine upon them. May they rest in peace. Amen.*

Fire of Love

"The Lord your God is a devouring fire." — *Deuteronomy 4:24*

"I see that this God of love hurls upon the souls certain burning rays so penetrating that they could consume soul and body if such were God's will" — St. Catherine of Genoa.

Reflection: Make an Offering of Actions today: "Eternal Father, by virtue of your generosity and love, I ask that you accept all my actions, and that you multiply their value in favor of every soul in purgatory. Through Christ Our Lord. Amen."

Eternal rest grant unto them, O Lord, and let perpetual light shine upon them. May they rest in peace. Amen.

Vanity of Vanities

Set me as a seal upon your heart, as a seal upon your arm; for
love is strong as death, jealousy is cruel as the grave. It flashes
of fire, a most vehement flame. — *Song of Solomon 8:6*

"The process of reforming and purifying which takes place in purgatory will be the more painful as resistance to grace has been more obstinate and prolonged" — Auguste Saudreau, French author.

Reflection: Many have a strong attachment to particular sins. Pray for the souls who have sinned the most in obstinacy.

Eternal rest grant unto them, O Lord, and let perpetual
light shine upon them. May they rest in peace. Amen.

Purify Your Heart

He who loves purity of heart, and whose speech is gracious,
will have the king as his friend. — Proverbs 22:11

"In purgatory is there given a conscious knowledge of God's exquisite purity in comparison to which all the highest ideals of our human conception of purity appear but foulness. Each holy soul learns to know itself as divine purity knows it" — St. Gertrude.

Purgatory exists because of God's love and His incomprehensible holiness. We need purification and healing because of our sin and selfishness. It is God's love that cleanses and purifies us to be able to stand before His presence. Let us, therefore, pray both for ourselves and for the holy souls.

Reflection: Pray with St. Gertrude: "Oh, my God, allow my sinful soul the contact of your infinite purity."

Eternal rest grant unto them, O Lord, and let perpetual
light shine upon them. May they rest in peace. Amen.

MAY 13

Purgatory Is Real

"Bear fruits that befit repentance." — Luke 3:8

"The Fátima Seer, Lucia, asked the Blessed Mother about their friend, Amelia, who died between the ages of 18 and 20. Our Lady's answer was startling. 'She will be in purgatory until the end of the world.' It was later learned that Amelia died in circumstances involving immoral behavior. Only God knows why she would be in purgatory until the end of the world. To be in purgatory, she must have been sincerely sorry for her sins when she died; however, she probably did not have sufficient time to make satisfaction for all the temporal punishment due to these sins. This is a powerful reminder to practice the virtues of a Christian life and do penance now while we have the chance, so that when we die we may go quickly to heaven" — Father Andrew Apostoli, Franciscan Friars of the Renewal, author.

Reflection: Make the Five First Saturdays (confession within eight days preceding or following the first Saturday, receive Holy Communion, recite the Rosary, spend fifteen minutes meditating on the mysteries of the Rosary) in reparation to the Immaculate Heart of Mary. Our Lady promises graces necessary for salvation. Ask Our Lady to include all family generations! Pray the Fátima Prayer: "O my Jesus, forgive us our sins, save us from the fires of hell. Lead all souls to heaven, especially those in most need of your mercy."

Eternal rest grant unto them, O Lord, and let perpetual light shine upon them. May they rest in peace. Amen.

Act of Perfect Love

Praise him, all his angels, praise him, all his host! — *Psalm 148:2*

The guardian angels render most valuable service to the souls in purgatory by suggesting to the Church Militant on earth the inspiration of praying for them and having Masses offered for their intention. These charitable and devoted angels never cease to assist the souls that God has committed to their care. When we concentrate our efforts on the deliverance of the souls in purgatory, our act of charity is turned into an act of perfect love of God in order to increase the number of the elect and to swell the chorus of praise and adoration that is offered in heaven to the majesty and perfection of the Most High. Everything done out of love of God has the power to expiate and destroy sin.

Reflection: Imitate your guardian angel in the things you do to help others, especially the holy souls.

Eternal rest grant unto them, O Lord, and let perpetual light shine upon them. May they rest in peace. Amen.

Cleansing Purges the Debt

Thus they reasoned, but they were led astray, for their wickedness blinded them, and they did not know the secret purpose of God, nor hope for the wages of holiness, nor discern the prize for blameless souls; for God created man for incorruption, and made him in the image of his own eternity. — Wisdom 2:21-23

"Who would dare to say that God would so unite with Himself any soul not perfectly spotless? Who will assert that Infinite Purity and Holiness would extend His arms and draw to His side, and press to His bosom, aught that is defiled or stained, or sinful, or impure? He knows little of God, who imagines that there can be any such union between light and darkness, between truth and falsehood, beauty and deformity ... till cleansed they can never enter heaven; never lose themselves in God or enjoy the society of the saints. Never while God continues to be what He is; while He is the infinite Sanctity, and the uncreated Goodness" — Monsignor John S. Vaughan, Irish author.

Reflection: Pray: "God be in my head, and in my understanding; God be in my eyes, and in my looking; God be in my mouth, and in my speaking; God be in my heart and in my thinking; God be at my end and my departing" (*Sarum Primer*, 1558).

Eternal rest grant unto them, O Lord, and let perpetual light shine upon them. May they rest in peace. Amen.

Sacrifice of St. Margaret of Cortona

"Judge not, and you will not be judged; condemn not, and you will not be condemned; forgive and you will be forgiven." — Luke 6:37

St. Margaret's parents rejected her and her son. Her stepmother showed little charity toward her. Undaunted she offered up all her sufferings, Masses, and Holy Communions for the repose of their souls. Because of this, Our Lord appeared to her and declared that due to her supplications, not only had she lessened the immense period of suffering her parents would have had to endure, but because of her sacrifices they were released from purgatory and were in heaven.

Reflection: Meditate on the wounds of Jesus. Generously love those who have little charity for you, and pray for those who persecute you.

Eternal rest grant unto them, O Lord, and let perpetual light shine upon them. May they rest in peace. Amen.

Paying Our Debt

"Truly, I say to you, you will never get out till you have paid the last penny." — Matthew 5:26

"After Vespers today, there was a procession to the cemetery. I could not go, because I was on duty at the gate. But that did not stop me at all from praying for the souls.

"As the procession was returning from the cemetery to the chapel, my soul felt the presence of many souls. I understood the great justice of God, how each one had to pay off the debt to the last cent" — St. Faustina (*Diary*, 1375).

Reflection: The souls in purgatory fix their gaze on you. It is through you that they enter heaven. Fix your gaze on the crucifix for their release.

Eternal rest grant unto them, O Lord, and let perpetual light shine upon them. May they rest in peace. Amen.

Unbearable Suffering

Save some, by snatching them out of the fire. — Jude 1:23

Living in a war-torn time period, Blessed Stanislaus Papcynzski — founder of the Marians of the Immaculate Conception — witnessed thousands of casualties on battlefields and also from dreaded plagues. He was deeply saddened to observe how many people died with no time to prepare to meet their maker.

After he experienced visions of the holy souls in purgatory, he was moved to engage in, and advocate for, prayer and penance on behalf of the dead. In one account, at a gathering of family, friends, and religious, Blessed Stanislaus had a profound mystical experience of the holy souls in Purgatory. He later told his confreres: "Pray, brethren, for the souls in purgatory, for they suffer unbearably." He then locked himself in his cell and spent three days praying for them.

Reflection: Blessed Stanislaus, pray for us and our beloved war dead!

Eternal rest grant unto them, O Lord, and let perpetual light shine upon them. May they rest in peace. Amen.

Cured a Bad Memory

The memory of the righteous is a blessing. — *Proverbs 10:7*

Pope Pius IX appointed Father Tomaso as a bishop of a diocese. Father Tomaso had a bad memory, which he thought would be a detriment to the office. The Pope said: "Your diocese is very small in comparison with the universal Church, which I carry on my shoulders. Your cares will be very light in comparison with mine. I, too, suffered from a very poor memory, but I promised to say a fervent prayer daily for the holy souls, who, in turn, have obtained for me an excellent memory. Do likewise, dear Father, and you will have cause to rejoice."

Reflection: Ask the holy souls to help you remember that our goal is eternity and to become holy here on earth.

*Eternal rest grant unto them, O Lord, and let perpetual
light shine upon them. May they rest in peace. Amen.*

Friends Forever

*There is nothing so precious as a faithful friend, and
no scales can measure his excellence. — Sirach 6:15*

"Perhaps we have few friends and few occasions of doing good. We envy
those known to all. It seems we may find few intimate friends in eternity;
few to whom we have done good on earth and who will thank us in eternity. Very well! Here is an easy means of surrounding ourselves in eternity
with many grateful friends, whose gratitude will augment our glory in
Paradise: we can make all the friends we wish in purgatory. What we shall
have done for them on earth shall establish between us and them, in eternity, a bond of unspeakable sweetness. God will reveal to them the good
we have done them, and they will know us to eternity as their benefactors.
We shall find them crowding around to intercede for us when we come
before the judgment seat of God" — Father Martin Jugie, Assumptionist,
Byzantine scholar, author.

Reflection: Develop eternal friendships with the souls through
prayer and good works for them.

---

*Eternal rest grant unto them, O Lord, and let perpetual
light shine upon them. May they rest in peace. Amen.*

Steps to Perfection

"Is not this the fast that I choose: to loose the bonds of wickedness, to undo the thongs of the yoke, to let the oppressed go free, and to break every yoke?" — Isaiah 58:6

"If you ask me what you are to do in order to be perfect, I say ... give your first thoughts to God; make a good visit to the Blessed Sacrament ... say the rosary well; be recollected; keep out bad thoughts; make your evening meditation well; examine yourself daily" – Blessed John Henry Newman.

Reflection: As you strive for perfection in light of these directives, implore the holy souls to help you succeed throughout the day.

Eternal rest grant unto them, O Lord, and let perpetual light shine upon them. May they rest in peace. Amen.

Good Passed On

The prayer of the humble pierces the clouds, and he will not be consoled until it reaches the Lord; he will not desist until the Most High visits him, and does justice for the righteous, and executes judgment. — Sirach 35:17

On August 24, 1590, St. Mary Magdalen de Pazzi's mother — a noble and devout woman — died. The saint saw the soul of her deceased parent in purgatory, but she also saw what great glory was soon prepared for her in heaven, for all the good that she had done and her generosity toward her neighbor. After fifteen days the saint saw the soul of her mother, for whom she had much prayed, and offered above all Holy Masses and Holy Communions and the Precious Blood of Jesus. The doctrine taught and lived by St. Mary Magdalen was the one promulgated by the Council of Trent, taught by the Church, and instituted for the supplications and the good that can be passed on by the living to the holy souls in purgatory.

And also for this: her work of persuasion and her example convinced many to follow her by laboring and praying for the holy souls in purgatory.

Reflection: Make an Act of Charity: "O my God, I love you above all things with my whole heart and soul because you are all good and worthy of all my love. I love my neighbor as myself for love of you. I forgive all who have injured me and ask pardon of all whom I have injured. Amen."

Eternal rest grant unto them, O Lord, and let perpetual light shine upon them. May they rest in peace. Amen.

The Faith of Our Ancestors

*Create in me a clean heart, O God, and put a new right
spirit within me. Cast me not away from thy presence, and
take not thy holy Spirit from me. — Psalm 51:10-11*

"If they have died repentant for their sins and having love of God, but
have not made satisfaction for things they have done or omitted by fruits
worthy of penance, then their souls, after death, are cleansed by the punishment of Purgatory; also ... the suffrages of the faithful still living are
efficacious in bringing them relief from such punishment, namely the Sacrifice of the Mass, prayers and almsgiving and other works of piety which,
in accordance with the designation of the Church, are customarily offered
by the faithful for each other" — Council of Florence.

"We constantly hold that purgatory exists, and that the souls of the
faithful there detained are helped by the prayers of the faithful" — Council
of Trent.

Reflection: When David atoned for his sins, God forgave him, but
also punished him for a time, to purify him. God is all merciful
and all just. Thank God for the doctrine of purgatory.

---

*Eternal rest grant unto them, O Lord, and let perpetual
light shine upon them. May they rest in peace. Amen.*

Catholicism on Purgatory

Always be prepared to make a defense to any one who
calls you to account for the hope that is in you, yet do it
with gentleness and reverence. — *1 Peter 3:15*

The *Catechism of the Catholic Church* teaches:

- "Each will be rewarded immediately after death in accordance with his works and faith" (n. 1021).
- Those who die in God's grace and friendship and are perfectly purified [with no need of purgatory] live forever with Christ" (n. 1023).
- "The Church formulated her doctrine of faith on Purgatory especially at the Councils of Florence and Trent" (n. 1031).
- "This teaching is also based on the practice of prayer for the dead, already mentioned in Sacred Scripture" (n. 1032).

Reflection: Read the *YOUCAT* (*Youth Catechism of the Catholic Church*) with your children, especially numbers 159-160 on purgatory. Pope Benedict XVI said: "You need to know what you believe and you need to know your faith with that same precision with which an IT specialist knows the inner workings of a computer. You need to understand it like a good musician knows the piece he is playing."

Eternal rest grant unto them, O Lord, and let perpetual
light shine upon them. May they rest in peace. Amen.

Feel the Burn

*In all your ways acknowledge him, and he will make straight
your paths. Be not wise in your own eyes; fear the LORD,
and turn away from evil. It will be healing to your flesh
and refreshment to your bones. — Proverbs 3:6-8*

One day while St. Mary Magdalen de Pazzi was praying in the garden of
the convent with the other religious, she became enraptured in ecstasy
and saw before her the pits of purgatory opening. She later shared that she
heard a voice beckoning her to follow and witness the pain that the holy
souls in purgatory had to endure. The voice explained that this invitation
was extended to her so that when she prayed for the souls, she would do so
relentlessly and compassionately. The sisters heard her say, "Yes, I will go."

Reflection: Give the hungry souls the fruit of your prayer — refreshment, light, and peace.

---

*Eternal rest grant unto them, O Lord, and let perpetual
light shine upon them. May they rest in peace. Amen.*

How Long in Purgatory?

Return, O LORD! How long? Have pity on thy servants. — Psalm 90:13

"The length of time a soul spends in purgatory depends on the number of their faults. The malice and deliberation with which these have been committed, the penance done or not done, the satisfaction made or not made for sins during life; on the suffrages offered for them after death.... This saving work is accomplished in union with the purifying power of God himself. The transforming power of God works in tandem with the repentant sinner. Living Christians and the saints in heaven support God with their prayers and spiritual assistance in this holy work. When this 'work' is done, heaven will open wide to welcome the soul" — Father Michael J. Taylor, S.J., Scripture scholar, author.

Reflection: Pray for the deceased who committed grievous sins and died without having done penance.

Eternal rest grant unto them, O Lord, and let perpetual light shine upon them. May they rest in peace. Amen.

Protectors and Escorts to Heaven

*Now to him who by the power at work within us is able
to do far more abundantly than all that we ask or think,
to him be glory in the church and in Christ Jesus to all
generations, for ever and ever. Amen. — Ephesians 3:20*

Venerable Frances of the Blessed Sacrament assures us that the holy souls assisted her in all dangers and disclosed to her the snares of the devil. A soul appeared to her and said: "Fear not, we will always defend you." Another soul assured her: "We pray daily for you; and as often as anyone remembers us, we also remember him and intercede for him with God. Especially do we implore for him the grace to serve God well and to die a happy death."

Reflection: What friends are the holy souls! Do all in your power to help these generous souls. Give thanks and praise to God for these faithful souls.

---

*Eternal rest grant unto them, O Lord, and let perpetual
light shine upon them. May they rest in peace. Amen.*

Offer a Sacrifice of Praise

"Praise the Lord of righteousness, and exalt the King of ages. I give him thanks in the land of my captivity, and I show his power and majesty to a nation of sinners. Turn back, you sinners, and do right before him; who knows if he will accept you and have mercy on you?" — *Tobit 13:6*

"The tongue that praises in the midst of afflictions is not inferior to the tongues of martyrs, and likely they may have both the same reward. If a man praise God, and give Him thanks in his sufferings, it is reputed as a kind of martyrdom; and would you have a martyr go to purgatory, he that finds heaven open, and ready to receive him?" — St. John Chrysostom.

Reflection: Pray for the souls most outstanding in the love of God.

Eternal rest grant unto them, O Lord, and let perpetual light shine upon them. May they rest in peace. Amen.

Prayer Gives You God

*Do not delay to turn to the Lord, nor postpone it from day to
day; for suddenly the wrath of the Lord will go forth, and at
the time of punishment you will perish.* — Sirach 5:7

"What years of purgatory will there be for those Christians who have no
difficulty at all in deferring their prayers to another time on the excuse
of having to do some pressing work! If we really desired the happiness of
possessing God, we should avoid the little faults as well as the big ones,
since separation from God is so frightful a torment to all these poor souls!"
— St. John Vianney.

Reflection: We become holy by prayer and sacrifice. Take the example of the men and women in the Bible who had the courage to live
the Gospel. Who are your favorites? Try to be like them.

---

*Eternal rest grant unto them, O Lord, and let perpetual
light shine upon them. May they rest in peace. Amen.*

Guardians from Heaven

Though she is but one, she can do all things, and while remaining in herself, she renews all things; in every generation she passes into holy souls and makes them friends of God and prophets. — Wisdom 7:27

"There are thousands of instances from which we may learn how efficiently the holy souls can obtain for us health in sickness, aid in poverty, relief in distress, counsel in doubt, and protection in danger. The more souls you release from purgatory, the more protectors you will have in heaven, where they will continually implore God for your welfare" — St. Gregory.

Reflection: When you pray for the holy souls, think of the gratitude of their guardian angels!

Eternal rest grant unto them, O Lord, and let perpetual light shine upon them. May they rest in peace. Amen.

MAY 31

Best Safeguard — Devotion to Our Lady

She is a tree of life to those who lay hold of her; those who
hold her fast are called happy. — Proverbs 3:18

"Devote and consecrate yourself entirely to Mary [Our Lady]. Make her a present of Masses, Communions, fasts; imitate her glorious virtues. If you do these things you need not fear purgatory. She will obtain for you such a measure of true contrition and conformity to God's will, so much patience in your last sickness, such holy and ardent desire to serve God, such profound humility, as to blot out of our souls what purgatory was to have done, and purify you in a present capacity to go directly into heaven and if an extraordinary pass should be necessary, who can better procure it for you than the Lady of the House, the Mother of the Judge, the Empress of Paradise, the Queen of the Universe?" — Etienne Binet, S.J., French author.

Reflection: Our Lady loves the holy souls as much as her Son, Jesus. Pray three times: "O Mary conceived without sin, pray for us who have recourse to Thee."

Eternal rest grant unto them, O Lord, and let perpetual
light shine upon them. May they rest in peace. Amen.

SUMMER

Purgatory is the wayfaring, as peaceful as it is painful, toward the Father's home.

Holy Angels, guardians of those blazing chasms, help me to call to mind those souls, so holy and resigned, from the bowels of the flames that torment them. Make us recognize among them our fathers, our mothers, our sisters, and brothers. Let their cries, so tender and heart-rending, capable of splitting the mountains and mollifying cruelty itself, reach and penetrate our ears.

— Father Charles Arminjon

Morning Offering Prayer

By St. Gertrude to the Sacred Heart of Jesus

My Good God! I now consecrate and offer to Thy greater glory every thought, word, action, pain, and suffering, the pulsations of my heart, and the motions of my senses, not only of this day, but all the days of my life; in union with the actions, and Passion and death of Jesus Christ, and His Sacred Humanity in Heaven; in union with Masses that have been said, are being said, and will be said to the end of time, throughout Christendom; in union with Jesus in the Blessed Sacrament in all the Tabernacles throughout the world; I offer them all for the intentions of the Sacred Heart of Jesus, and for the relief of the suffering souls in purgatory.

(Pray daily for the holy souls during the month of June, which is dedicated to the Sacred Heart.)

JUNE 1

You Are Needed

Pray at all times in the Spirit, with all prayer and supplication.
To that end keep alert with all perseverance, making
supplication for all the saints. — Ephesians 6:18

"Enter into purgatory often, because [the souls] need you there" — Jesus
to St. Faustina (*Diary*, 1738).

Reflection: When you console the beloved souls, you console the
heart of Jesus. Pray with St. Faustina: "Most merciful Jesus, You
Yourself have said that You desire mercy; so I bring into the abode
of Your Most Compassionate Heart the souls in Purgatory, souls
who are very dear to You, and yet, who must make retribution to
Your justice. May the streams of Blood and Water which gushed
forth from Your Heart put out the flames of purgatory, that there,
too, the power of Your mercy may be praised" (*Diary*, 1227).

Eternal rest grant unto them, O Lord, and let perpetual
light shine upon them. May they rest in peace. Amen.

The Soul's Salvation

He saved us, not because of deeds done by us in righteousness, but in virtue of his own mercy, by the washing of regeneration and renewal in the Holy Spirit. — Titus 3:5

"How holy and happy to contemplate this view of purgatory. The soul is saved, sure of eternal glories. She is impeccable, conformed in grace, accepts, embraces, kisses the chains of Divine love that God's sweet mercy presents to her" — Abbé Cloquet, French author.

Reflection: We depend on the "sweet mercy" of the Lord for our salvation. Practice extending mercy to someone who has treated you badly.

Eternal rest grant unto them, O Lord, and let perpetual light shine upon them. May they rest in peace. Amen.

Two-Sided Devotion

More than that, we rejoice in our sufferings, knowing that
suffering produces endurance, and endurance produces
character, and character produces hope. — Romans 5:3-4

"A Jesuit Polish saint, Andrew Bobola had successfully converted thousands of Orthodox back to Catholic unity. The Russian Cossacks tracked him down. After hours of torture and before he died, he kept praying, 'Lord, keep me faithful. Save me from the fires of hell.' He was afraid of weakening under torment and denying his faith. Even the saints at times could be so tempted that the love of God would not be enough to sustain them in resisting temptation. Even the saints at times need the fear of God's punishment to remain in His grace.

"What sustained him? The fear of an eternal loss of God in hell. We need that same motivation, my friends. I cannot think of a more salutary and inspiring way to practice charity than to develop an extraordinary concern for the poor souls. Pray for them.... The beauty of our patient endurance of suffering on earth is that it has a two-fold merit. One for ourselves: it purifies us. It expiates our own punishment due to sin and contributes to the release from and mitigation of pain in purgatory" — Father John A. Hardon, S.J., theologian, author.

Reflection: Practice daily the virtues of charity, patience, humility of heart. Reap the fruits of peace in your heart, hearing the voice of God and harvesting the graces and rewards for you and the most grateful souls.

Eternal rest grant unto them, O Lord, and let perpetual
light shine upon them. May they rest in peace. Amen.

Better to Please God

"Father, if thou art willing, remove this cup from me; nevertheless not my will, but thine, be done." — Luke 22:42

"To please God is a better thing than to avoid sufferings; yet a man who keeps his satisfaction and indulgences to himself, does so from a desire of avoiding sufferings; whereas, he who offers them all for the souls in purgatory, thereby makes himself dearer to God, by a refinement of love, by this heroic exercise of mercy and charity which he is not bound to do, but does so out of the sweet freedom of his own will" — Father Frederick Faber, convert, English hymn writer, theologian, author.

Reflection: Offer your penances for the holy servants of God. Penance can include being faithful to your state in life, faithful to God, faithful to His decrees and to love holy Mother Church. It is not difficult.

Eternal rest grant unto them, O Lord, and let perpetual light shine upon them. May they rest in peace. Amen.

JUNE 5

Second Guardian Angel

"Ask, and it will be given you; seek, and you will find;
knock, and it will be opened to you." — Matthew 7:7

"The souls in purgatory are holy, and dear to God. Charity urges them to love us, and they know at least, in a general way, to what dangers we are exposed; and what need we have of the Divine assistance. Why then would they not pray for us?" — Francisco Suarez, S.J., Spanish philosopher, theologian.

Reflection: The holy souls are like our second guardian angels. Just as we show our concern for them and help them with our prayers, they assist us with theirs.

Eternal rest grant unto them, O Lord, and let perpetual
light shine upon them. May they rest in peace. Amen.

Grab the Grace of Indulgences

Those who trust in him will understand truth, and the faithful will abide with him in love, because grace and mercy are upon his elect, and he watches over his holy ones. — Wisdom 3:9

St. Alphonsus was so solicitous about gaining indulgences that, after his death, several indulgenced articles were found on him. He had always worn them wherever he went in order to gain as many indulgences as possible.

Reflection: A popular indulgenced prayer is the Eternal Rest Prayer (see below). Be fervent in praying it throughout the day.

Eternal rest grant unto them, O Lord, and let perpetual light shine upon them. May they rest in peace. Amen.

Heavenly Refiner

Like gold in the furnace he tried them, and like a sacrificial burnt offering he accepted them. — Wisdom 3:6

"What a beautiful thought contained in these words. It is said that the refiner of silver and gold watches the vapors arising from the melting-pot until his own countenance is reflected as from a mirror brightly shining on the surface of the seething and melting mass. Then he knows that his work is done. Does not the heavenly Refiner do the same?" — Paul von Keppler, bishop (of Rottenburg, Germany), author.

Reflection: Can others see the Lord reflected in us? How can we bring this image into clearer focus?

Eternal rest grant unto them, O Lord, and let perpetual light shine upon them. May they rest in peace. Amen.

Purity Through Prayer

Thou who art of purer eyes than to behold evil. — *Habakkuk 1:13*

"We must say many prayers for the souls of the faithful departed, for one must be so pure to enter heaven" — St. John Vianney.

Reflection: We cannot begin to comprehend God's purity. In imitation of God's holy purity, plead with Him to be pure in thought, word, and deed for the sake of the suffering souls.

Eternal rest grant unto them, O Lord, and let perpetual light shine upon them. May they rest in peace. Amen.

Unspeakable Holiness

The LORD our God is holy! — Psalm 99:9

During her agony, God allowed St. Teresa of Ávila to see His holiness as the angels and the saints see Him in heaven, which caused her so much dread that her sisters, seeing her trembling and extraordinarily agitated, spoke to her, weeping: "Ah, Mother, what has happened to you; surely you do not fear death after so many penances and such abundant and bitter tears?" St. Teresa replied that she did not fear death. The sisters continued to ask. "Do you fear your sins? Hell?" St. Teresa continued to say no. Then she said: "Oh, my sisters, it is the holiness of God. My God, have pity on me!"

Reflection: Pray: "Lamb of God, you take away the sins of the world, have mercy on us. Lamb of God, you take away the sins of the world, have mercy on us. Lamb of God, you take away the sins of the world, grant us peace."

Eternal rest grant unto them, O Lord, and let perpetual light shine upon them. May they rest in peace. Amen.

The Goodness and Mercy of God

"I will make all my goodness pass before you, and will proclaim before you my name 'The LORD.'" — *Exodus 33:19*

"God is so infinitely desirable that His absence is such an inexpressible torture. It is only because joy is so intense in heaven, that pain is so dire in purgatory. Were God less attractive, less lovable, less beautiful, the privation of His presence would be less agonizing" — Monsignor John S. Vaughan, Irish author.

Reflection: God rewards us for even the smallest action. He does so over and above all that we could desire. Do not neglect to do even ordinary tasks for the benefit of the holy souls.

Eternal rest grant unto them, O Lord, and let perpetual light shine upon them. May they rest in peace. Amen.

JUNE 11

Glory to God

Bear one another's burdens. — *Galatians 6:2*

"Anna Mary Taigi, a holy woman of Rome, was also privileged often to see released souls, who came to thank her. One day she intended to receive Holy Communion in the basilica of St. John Lateran, and to offer it for a certain deceased person.

"During the first Mass at which she assisted, and which was celebrated by her confessor, she was suddenly attacked with a great depression of spirit joined with severe bodily pains. Nevertheless she continued in prayer and offered up her illness in atonement to divine justice. Then Cardinal Pedicini began his Mass. At the *Gloria* the saintly woman was suddenly seized with the great supernatural joy and consolation. Then a soul just released from Purgatory appeared to her and said: 'I thank thee, my sister, for thy compassion. I will remember thee at the throne of God; for thanks to thy prayer I now go to enter heaven, where I shall be in bliss forever'" — Father Albert Bessieres, S.J., author.

Reflection: Next time you are at Mass offer the *Gloria* for the holy souls to give honor, praise, and glory to God.

Eternal rest grant unto them, O Lord, and let perpetual light shine upon them. May they rest in peace. Amen.

Treasures for the Souls

*"If any man would come after me, let him deny himself and
take up his cross daily and follow me." — Luke 9:23*

During the life of Venerable Mary D'Antigna, a deceased nun of her monastery appeared to her and requested that the nuns pray the devotion of the Stations of the Cross for her and for the other souls. Mary then heard the voice of Jesus in her heart saying that the prayer of the Way of the Cross is very helpful to the holy souls and asking her to tell her sisters how much good they do with this devotion and the treasures they store up when they offer it for the holy souls in purgatory.

Reflection: Make the Way of the Cross for the soul of your mother, father, sister, brother, or friend. The stations elicit sympathy and compassion. The holy wounds of Jesus are the treasure of treasures for the holy souls.

---

*Eternal rest grant unto them, O Lord, and let perpetual
light shine upon them. May they rest in peace. Amen.*

JUNE 13

Please the Angels of God

*"I brought a reminder of your prayer before
the Holy One." — Tobit 12:12*

In the Book of Tobit, Tobit, a pious man, often buried the dead, even the enemies of the Hebrews. Once he got up from dinner in order to do so. The Archangel Raphael was so grateful for this mercy of Tobit that he assisted Tobit's son and restored the old man's sight. He gave Tobit to understand that his tearful prayers and his mercy in burying the dead pleased him so much that Raphael himself would present Tobit's prayers to God.

Reflection: Let us thank our guardian angels for the love they give to us. They never take their eyes off us. Pray the Guardian Angel Prayer (see page 391).

*Eternal rest grant unto them, O Lord, and let perpetual
light shine upon them. May they rest in peace. Amen.*

JUNE 14

From an Angel's Hands to God

*Of the angels he says, "Who makes his angels winds,
and his servants flames of fire." — Hebrews 1:7*

"It pleases God that our prayers are presented to Him by the angels. That an angel comes to gather our prayers, and they mount, from the hand of the angel even to the face of God. See in what manner it serves them to be presented by so pure a hand. They mount from the hand of the angel because that angel, joining itself to us and aiding our feeble prayers, lends them its wings to raise them, its strength to sustain them, its fervor to vivify them" — St. John of Ávila.

Reflection: Your prayers and services for the dead are most pleasing to the angels of God. Give your prayers over to your guardian angel.

---

*Eternal rest grant unto them, O Lord, and let perpetual
light shine upon them. May they rest in peace. Amen.*

Purgatory Today

"Do not come near; put off your shoes from your feet, for the place
on which you are standing is holy ground." — Exodus 3:5

"One must be absolutely pure to enter heaven. The beatific vision is granted to a Christian only if he has attained a state of perfect purity. Where this is not perfect, the imputability of sin ... requires a painful purification which fully conforms the human will to the divine order, once and for all cleansing it of stains acquired during the earthly pilgrimage. Scripture implies consequences as the result of one's own sins. In 2 Samuel 12 there is a typical cause of the separability between guilt and punishment, for God's pardon (v. 13) does not exempt David from the necessity of suffering for his sin (v. 14).

"David said to Nathan, 'I have sinned against the Lord.' And Nathan said to David, 'The Lord has put away your sin; you shall not die. Nevertheless, because by this deed you have utterly scorned the Lord, the child that is born to you shall die.' Consequently, this situation would require the addition of certain purification after death.... God in His gentle love as a father uses the suffering of delay in order to be able to give us the fullness of joy, and He makes up for man's faults and completes the work that man has not finished in his earthly life" — Kenneth J. Baker, S.J., author.

Reflection: We cannot assume that a loved one has avoided purgatory, so let us prayerfully remember our beloved dead.

Eternal rest grant unto them, O Lord, and let perpetual
light shine upon them. May they rest in peace. Amen.

Waiting at the Gates

Our feet have been standing within your gates,
O Jerusalem! — Psalm 122:2

St. Pio of Pietrelcina — Padre Pio — was particularly concerned that everybody should enter Paradise. He said: "I have made a covenant with God. After my soul is purified in purgatory and is then worthy to enter Heaven, I will only stand at its gates and not enter until I have seen the last of my brothers and spiritual children enter before me."

Reflection: Pray this prayer by Padre Pio: "We believe, dear Jesus, that nothing defiled can enter heaven. Make us, dear Savior, undefiled so that as we approach the dawn of eternity we may enter that heaven you have prepared for us — we beg, dear Lord, immediately. Amen." Enroll your family as spiritual children of Padre Pio. He promised not to enter Paradise until all his spiritual children entered. (See page 395 for more information.)

Eternal rest grant unto them, O Lord, and let perpetual
light shine upon them. May they rest in peace. Amen.

Fire of Divine Love

We love because he first loved us. — 1 John 4:19

"The man who is inflamed with the fire of divine love is as indifferent to glory and ignominy as if he were alone and unseen on this earth. He spurns all temptations. He is no more troubled by pincers, gridirons, or racks than if these sufferings were endured in a body other than his own. What is full of sweetness for the world has no attraction for him, no taste; he is no more liable to be captivated by some evil attachment than is gold, seven times tested, liable to be tarnished by rust. Such are, even on this earth, the effects of divine love when it firmly takes hold of a soul" — St. John Chrysostom.

Reflection: Pray: "Holy souls, heirs of heaven, help me deal with all that's distressing me today."

Eternal rest grant unto them, O Lord, and let perpetual light shine upon them. May they rest in peace. Amen.

Cleanse Our Souls

"For the life of the flesh is in the blood; and I have given it for you upon the altar to make atonement for your souls; for it is the blood that makes atonement, by reason of the life." — Leviticus 17:11

"For when St. Gertrude, at the Elevation of the Adorable Host, fervently prayed: 'Holy Lord God, I offer Thee this Sacred Host for the remission of my sins,' these words were effectual not merely to cleanse her soul from the stains it had contracted, but to render it worthy to be admitted to the bosom of God the Father" — St. Gertrude.

Reflection: At the elevation of the Sacred Body and Blood of Jesus at Mass, beg the Lord's forgiveness for any sins of omission or commission.

Eternal rest grant unto them, O Lord, and let perpetual light shine upon them. May they rest in peace. Amen.

JUNE 19

Love, Not Punishment

Let not loyalty and faithfulness forsake you; bind them about your neck, write them on the tablet of your heart. So you will find favor and good repute in the sight of God and man. — Proverbs 3:3-4

"This work of purgatory can be called 'punishment' only in the sense that it will be spiritually and psychologically demanding, as the acquisition of virtue always is" — Father Michael J. Taylor, S.J., Scripture scholar, author.

Reflection: Jesus said to St. Catherine of Siena: "You test the virtue of patience in yourself when your neighbors insult you. Your humility is tested by the proud, your faith by the unfaithful, your hope by the person who has no hope. Your justice is tried by the unjust, your compassion by the cruel, and your gentleness and kindness by the wrathful. Your neighbors are the channel through which all your virtues are tested and come to birth, just as the evil gives birth to all their vices through their neighbors."

Ask the holy souls to help you to determine a specific virtue you need to develop in honor of them.

Eternal rest grant unto them, O Lord, and let perpetual light shine upon them. May they rest in peace. Amen.

JUNE 20

Holy Fire

Set me as a seal upon your heart, as a seal upon your arm;
for love is strong as death.... Its flashes are flashes of fire,
a most vehement flame. — *Song of Solomon 8:6*

Does fire really exist in purgatory? The Catholic Church teaches that the soul undergoes purification. A suffering of the soul resembles expiating and in some way a purifying action of fire. Spiritual writers speak of the fire of purgatory, but this is a symbolic and metaphorical image of the purification sinful souls are in need of in order to overcome the debilitating effects of sin. In the Middle Ages, the primary image or motif for purification was fire. God's love is referred to as being like fire. It also represents God's efforts to purify and prepare these souls for heaven. A literal fire destroys the evil in things, so "God's fire" destroys the moral evil that remains in the soul at death. It cleanses and purifies souls of all the elements of evil that can impair their capacity for glory. For Jews and early Christians fire was seen as a symbolic image of God's judgment.

Reflection: Let your heart burn for love of the holy souls.

Eternal rest grant unto them, O Lord, and let perpetual
light shine upon them. May they rest in peace. Amen.

Agony of Love

*LORD, all my longing is known to thee, my sighing
is not hidden from thee. — Psalm 38:9*

"St. Teresa of Ávila was once granted to see the sacred hand of Jesus. It threw her in ecstasy and caused her to swoon away with transports of delight. To see God Himself in His own unfading beauty, infinite and uncreated, would wrench the very heart from our bosom, and enkindle a fire of desire throughout every fiber of our being, more fierce than the sun at noon. It is this which must take place when a soul enters purgatory. Death comes ... and the instant the child of the most High looks up into the face of its heavenly father, its whole heart aches for Him. If its longing is denied, it suffers purgatorial pains. A longing-deep insatiable desire fills his soul ... a burning sorrow, a kind of spiritual fever, which cannot be adequately expressed by the human word fire" — Father Martin Jugie, Assumptionist, Byzantine scholar, author; and Monsignor John S. Vaughan, Irish author.

Reflection: Beg the Holy Spirit, the fire of Divine love, to burn in your heart a fiery passion for Jesus.

---

*Eternal rest grant unto them, O Lord, and let perpetual
light shine upon them. May they rest in peace. Amen.*

JUNE 22

Wounds of Love

*My soul longs, yea, faints for the courts of the LORD; my heart
and flesh sing for joy to the living God.* — Psalm 84:2

Love can sometimes produce effects in the human breast that recall those
of material fire. We read this in the lives of certain saints. The Holy Spirit
comes to them as a wellspring of intolerable love, as a consuming fire, as
a love wound of death and life. St. Mary Magdalene de Pazzi was heard
to cry: "O Love, you cause me to consume and melt. You cause me to die,
and yet to live." We often hear the common phrase: "I have a burning
desire" for such and such.

St. Philip Neri could not support the ardor of the fire that the love
of God kindled within him. While fervently praying in the catacombs
around 1545, he experienced an ecstasy when his heart was enlarged; two
ribs were broken to make room for his enlarged heart, which was filled
with spirit, love, joy, and cheer. To ease the burning he would uncover his
breast in the cold.

St. Faustina said: "I felt some kind of fire in my heart.... An extraordinary suffering pervades my soul, together with a joy I cannot compare to
anything" (*Diary*, 432).

Blessed Mary of Providence shared: "Today I feel as though my hands
were on fire. I am burning! ... My God, I burn with love for You! I feel
within me an inconceivable hunger and thirst for God."

Reflection: Ask God for the gift of love.

---

*Eternal rest grant unto them, O Lord, and let perpetual
light shine upon them. May they rest in peace. Amen.*

Final Agony

May the Lord grant him to find mercy from the
Lord on that Day. — 2 Timothy 1:18

"Pray for the dying. People all over the world die unprepared every day. We should come to their aid by our prayers. This prayer will give us the grace of a happy death, to die in the state of grace. It will compensate for our lack of charity towards our neighbor" — St. Louis Guanella, founder of the Pious Union of St. Joseph in 1924.

Reflection: Pray this prayer daily as a means to avoid purgatory: "Divine Heart of Jesus, convert sinners, save the dying, deliver the souls in purgatory."

Eternal rest grant unto them, O Lord, and let perpetual
light shine upon them. May they rest in peace. Amen.

Our Lady's Gifts

*And a great portent appeared in heaven, a woman clothed
with the sun, with the moon under her feet, and on her
head a crown of twelve stars. — Revelation 12:1*

"Imagine how happy Jesus is when souls are presented to Him by His Mother. This is because she covers them with her beauty, gives them the perfume of her holiness, the innocence of her purity, the white robe of her charity and, where there remains some stain, she runs her motherly hand over it to wipe it away and to give you that brightness which makes it possible for you to enter into the eternal happiness of paradise. Blessed are they who die under our Lady's mantle close to her Immaculate Heart. They find rest in their labors, and their good deeds will follow them" — Dr. Thomas Petrisko, author.

Reflection: Pray with the heart in adoration and supplication. Pray with the heart and from the heart in all your prayers. It will surely be pleasing to God.

---

*Eternal rest grant unto them, O Lord, and let perpetual
light shine upon them. May they rest in peace. Amen.*

JUNE 25

Mother Mary Is with You

*"And why is this granted me, that the mother
of my Lord should come to me?"* — Luke 1:43

If we pray for the most abandoned souls in purgatory the Blessed Mother
will remember us and will answer that verse "now and at the hour of our
death" that we pray in the Hail Mary.

Reflection: Meditate on the Rosary every day. The Rosary works
miracles in our lives and in the world.

---

*Eternal rest grant unto them, O Lord, and let perpetual
light shine upon them. May they rest in peace. Amen.*

Pray With the Heart

For the word of God is living and active, sharper than any two-edged sword, piercing to the division of soul and spirit, of joints and marrow, and discerning the thoughts and intentions of the heart. — Hebrews 4:12

St. Marie-Victoire Thérèse Couderc — who founded the Society of Our Lady of the Cenacle in 1826 and offered herself as a victim-soul for the souls in purgatory — said, "I heard them say all together the *Miserere*, the *Te Deum* and other liturgical prayers in accents of adoration and supplication such as earth has never heard." The harmony and reverence of their prayer filled her soul with an unutterable sense of the majesty of God and their own personal holiness.

Reflection: Pray with St. Thérèse Couderc: "Eyes of Mary, turn toward me. Lips of Mary, pray for me. Heart of Mary, love Jesus for me."

Eternal rest grant unto them, O Lord, and let perpetual light shine upon them. May they rest in peace. Amen.

Confident Prayer

"Those who have done good, to the resurrection of life, and those who have done evil, to the resurrection of judgment." — *John 5:29*

"If you deliver one soul from purgatory, you can say with confidence, 'Heaven is mine'" — St. Leonard of Port Maurice.

Reflection: The soul is in *exile*, banished from her native land to a distant shore in purification of her faults; the soul is also a *prisoner* deprived of liberty, helpless until time and suffering are aided by our Masses, prayers, and acts of piety. The poor soul is also a *widow*, and the trials and sorrows of widowhood are added to her other afflictions. Jesus Christ, her loving spouse, to whom she is united by the bonds of a holy union, is far from her, and in silence and sorrow she mourns His absence. Like the virgin daughter of Zion, "She weeps bitterly in the night, tears on her cheeks; among all her lovers she has none to comfort her" (Lam 1:2). Pray for the deliverance from purgatory of one particular soul, either known or unknown to you.

Eternal rest grant unto them, O Lord, and let perpetual light shine upon them. May they rest in peace. Amen.

Mary, Queen of Purgatory

"Behold, your mother!" — John 19:27

"The Holy Virgin does not love purgatory. It is a place of sorrow. I love to pray for the souls in purgatory, and the most Holy Virgin chides me because I do not ask sufficient for them. She said: 'I await graces for these souls — the graces which I did not dare to ask'" — Père Jean Édouard Lamy, mystic, founder of the Religious Congregation of the Servants of Jesus and Mary, author.

Reflection: Turn everything over to Our Blessed Mother. After all, who knows better than Mother?

Eternal rest grant unto them, O Lord, and let perpetual light shine upon them. May they rest in peace. Amen.

Hasten to the Altar

"Truly, truly, I say to you, unless you eat the flesh of the Son of man and drink his blood, you have no life in you." — John 6:53

To render her prayers more valuable for the holy souls, St. Margaret of Cortona would add to them the most Holy Communion.

Reflection: "There is no surer pledge or clearer sign of this great hope in the new heavens and new earth 'in which righteousness dwells,' than the Eucharist. Every time this mystery is celebrated, 'the work of our redemption is carried on' and we 'break the one bread that provides the medicine of immortality, the antidote for death, and the food that makes us live forever in Jesus Christ'" (*Catechism of the Catholic Church,* n. 1405). Make a nine-day novena of Holy Communions for the holy soul who is most like yourself. Either attend Mass nine days in a row or Sunday Mass for nine weeks, offering your Holy Communion for that holy soul.

Eternal rest grant unto them, O Lord, and let perpetual light shine upon them. May they rest in peace. Amen.

Spiritual Surgery

The point is this: he who sows sparingly will also reap sparingly, and he who sows bountifully will also reap bountifully. — *2 Corinthians 9:6*

"St. Antoninus had a vision of a soul who had been dead for some time. Though many Masses were offered for his soul, he said: 'My brother, all the Masses and prayers that have been offered up for me have been given to those souls who I should have prayed for in a special way, but did not do it. I shall have to remain in purgatory until I have satisfied the justice of God. No relief has been given to me. *They* are relieved instead of me.

"'Pray for me that God may forgive my neglect. Preach to the people everywhere to pray for the souls of the departed, lest, when they die, God may treat them as He has treated me'" — Sister M. Emmanuel, O.S.B., author.

Reflection: Do not neglect the holy souls, lest you find yourself neglected. Offer a special prayer for the souls for whom you are most bound to pray.

Eternal rest grant unto them, O Lord, and let perpetual light shine upon them. May they rest in peace. Amen.

God Is the Center

Draw near to God and he will draw near to you. — James 4:8

"All holy souls — all souls, that is to say, which are enlightened by truth and guided by charity, are in communion. Even here below, without knowing it, they are linked to one another, they are members of a society of which God is the center, the life, the light, the beauty, and the bliss. They help one another by their prayers and good works; they suffer for one another's sake; they are like the stones of which a church is built, which are hidden from one another, yet support one another from the foundation to the roof. Once they reach their goal, which is God, they see themselves and all things else in God, just as here below, although but imperfectly, see the world in the sunlight. There, in that expanse which has neither limit nor shade, they meet and enjoy one another in a far closer embrace than even during their earthly pilgrimage.... Those who were loved on earth will wonder at finding how slight a thing that love was, and true love will come to them as a revelation equaled only by their former ignorance. In purgatory, however, in which souls are kept away from God, they only have the hope of that boundless and everlasting communion. Perhaps they may be able to see souls nearest them, if any are nearer than others; or perhaps they will mourn awhile in lonely seclusion, till their expiation shall be accomplished and they shall be admitted to the light" — Father Henri-Dominque Lacordaire, O.P., who re-founded the Order of Preachers in France after the French Revolution.

Reflection: Put God at the center of your life. He is your greatest friend.

Eternal rest grant unto them, O Lord, and let perpetual light shine upon them. May they rest in peace. Amen.

The Beauty of Prayer

*And another angel came and stood at the altar with a golden
censer; and he was given much incense to mingle with the prayers
of all the saints upon the golden altar before the throne; and
the smoke of the incense rose with the prayers of the saints from
the hand of the angel before God.* — *Revelation 8:3-4*

"The Church Triumphant prostrates themselves before the Lamb, each
one having a harp and phials of gold full of perfumes, which are the
prayers of the saints. The Church Militant supplies the perfume of our
prayers. The angels and saints receive them in their golden phials and in
turn augment the value in refining the aroma so that, united to the perfume of their own intercession, it may arise more sweetly to the throne of
God. The elect receive them, join to them the gold of their glory and of
their intercession and thus greatly increase their efficacy" — Mother Mary
of St. Austin, Helpers of the Holy Souls, author.

Reflection: Say this intention throughout the day: "For the love of
Jesus and Mary and the relief of the holy souls."

---

*Eternal rest grant unto them, O Lord, and let perpetual
light shine upon them. May they rest in peace. Amen.*

JULY 3

Sacrament of Fire

"Every one will be salted with fire." — *Mark 9:49*

"According to Father Frederick Faber, the extreme severity of purgatory would be inconceivable if we did not believe in a vast number of souls saved, and saved, too, with very imperfect dispositions. In the presence of this system of expiation — which we might almost call an eighth sacrament, the sacrament of fire, for souls on which the seven real sacraments have not sufficed to confer perfect purity — must we not admit that it is an invention of God, in order to multiply the fruits of the Passion of Our Savior, established for the benefit of that great multitude of souls, who were to die in His love, though their love for Him was imperfect? Purgatory, indeed, gives us a sort of proof, both of the mercy of God and of our own cowardice: that is why souls are sent there by thousands, to receive from the flames the beauty they do not possess" — Father Henri Faure, S.M., French author.

Reflection: Change your life. Convert, pray, fast. Don't wait.

---

*Eternal rest grant unto them, O Lord, and let perpetual
light shine upon them. May they rest in peace. Amen.*

JULY 4

Pain of Sense

*"If then your whole body is full of light, having no
part dark, it will be wholly bright, as when a lamp
with its rays gives you light." — Luke 11:36*

The pain suffered by the souls in purgatory involves the pain of purification. Catherine of Genoa says that "the love of God directs towards the soul certain burning rays of light, which seem penetrating and powerful enough to annihilate, not merely the body, but were it possible, the very soul itself. They work in two ways: they purify and they annihilate. Now the soul cannot be annihilated so far as it is in God, but only in itself; and the more it is purified, the more it annihilates itself, until at last it becomes quite pure and rests in God. It becomes impassible because there is nothing left to be consumed. And if in this state of purity it was kept in the fire, it would feel no pain."

Reflection: Purification is necessary for our spiritual healing. Reject things you are attached to but hurt your spiritual life.

---

*Eternal rest grant unto them, O Lord, and let perpetual
light shine upon them. May they rest in peace. Amen.*

The Power of the Mass

*O Lord Almighty, God of Israel, hear now the prayer of the dead
of Israel and of the sons of those who sinned before thee, who did
not heed the voice of the Lord their God, so that calamities have
clung to us. Remember not the iniquities of our fathers, but in this
crisis remember thy power and thy name. For thou art the Lord
our God, and thee, O Lord, will we praise. — Baruch 3:4-6*

"The fruit of the Mass is exceedingly bountiful, for it renders us participators in the superabundant riches of Christ's merits and satisfaction for sin. Such is the power of Holy Mass that our sins melt away before it as wax before the fire, and the penalties we have incurred are turned aside from us" — Father Theodor Stratius, author.

Reflection: By assisting devoutly at Mass, we render the sacred humanity of Our Lord the greatest homage. He makes up for many negligences and omissions. We should pray like this at the beginning of Mass: "O most just God, with contrite heart and steadfast hope, I lay my sins upon this sacred altar, in order that they may be consumed by the flames of Your divine Charity, purged away by the Precious Blood of Jesus, and fully atoned for by His infinite merits. Amen."

---

*Eternal rest grant unto them, O Lord, and let perpetual
light shine upon them. May they rest in peace. Amen.*

Sweetness Before the Sovereign Judge

"For almsgiving delivers from death, and it will
purge away every sin." — *Tobit 12:9*

"Almsgiving is a friend of God; she is always found near Him, obtains favors agreeable to Him, breaks the chains of sin, dissipates darkness, stifles the flames of passion, and opens the gate of heaven. Those who have charge of her respect her as a queen; they ask not who she is or whom she seeks: all go to meet and receive her with joy. She is pure; she has golden wings and garments of marvelous beauty; her countenance is full of sweetness; when we appear before the tribunal of the sovereign Judge, she flies to meet us, and covers us with the protection of her wings. The swiftness of her wings carries her in a moment to the throne of God" — St. John Chrysostom.

Reflection: All you do for the poor sufferers, do with great joy and humility.

Eternal rest grant unto them, O Lord, and let perpetual
light shine upon them. May they rest in peace. Amen.

JULY 7

Holy Sorrow

"Therefore I will not restrain my mouth; I will speak in the anguish of my spirit; I will complain in the bitterness of my soul." — Job 7:11

"Who will describe their anguish, who will express their bitterness? Their love is the measure of their distress; and in so far as a finite nature will permit, their love is proportioned to its object; and its object is the infinite God. God the unlimited, the boundless, the only absolute beauty. To measure their grief, then, we must measure God's loveliness; to gauge the depth of their pain we must sound the bottomless abyss of God's perfections. But who can do this? Let it suffice, then, to say that their pains are beyond all computation, and exceed all thought and power of utterance. Such, then, is the doctrine of the Church of Christ." — Monsignor John S. Vaughan, Irish author.

Reflection: These silent sufferers do not want us to go to purgatory. They know by their own experiences the trials and temptations in life. They want us to understand the malice of sin. They are near us and watch over us with care. Do a daily examination of conscience about the sins, faults, and omissions of the past day. Make an Act of Contrition (see page 390).

Eternal rest grant unto them, O Lord, and let perpetual light shine upon them. May they rest in peace. Amen.

The Compassionate Hand

O God, thou art my God, I seek thee, my soul
thirsts for thee; my flesh faints for thee, as in a dry
and weary land where no water is. — Psalm 63:1

"Who is so tormented by hunger and thirst, who is so naked, so sick, so closely imprisoned as the souls in purgatory? They sigh day and night for the Bread of Angels, they long to refresh themselves from the fountain of the living water; banished from paradise, they have nothing to clothe them but the pains of purgatory; they suffer and groan, shut up in the prison of purgatory. To devote oneself to the relief of the souls in purgatory is equivalent to doing all the acts of mercy which Our Lord praises so highly, and so all our actions are transformed into works of charity, and all have the special merits of that excellent virtue" — St. Francis de Sales.

Reflection: The holy souls lament because they are not assisted. Open your heart. Offer your service for them. Do a kindly deed on their behalf for the elderly.

Eternal rest grant unto them, O Lord, and let perpetual
light shine upon them. May they rest in peace. Amen.

JULY 9

Longing for God

*Whom have I in heaven but thee? And there is nothing
upon earth that I desire besides thee.* — *Psalm 73:25*

"This evening, one of the deceased sisters came and asked me for one day
of fasting and to offer all my [spiritual] exercises on that day for her. I
answered that I would. From early morning on the following day, I offered
everything for her intention. During Holy Mass I had a brief experience
of her torment. I experienced such intense hunger for God, that I seemed
to be dying of the desire to become united with Him. This lasted only a
short time, but I understood what the longing of the souls in purgatory
was like" — St. Faustina (*Diary*, 1185-1186).

Reflection: Pray the Eternal Rest Prayer (see below) before and after
meals.

*Eternal rest grant unto them, O Lord, and let perpetual
light shine upon them. May they rest in peace. Amen.*

A Prayer for Each Fault

*Give graciously to all the living, and withhold
not kindness from the dead. — Sirach 7:33*

"Do we forget to pray for the souls in purgatory? Perhaps a handy reminder such as the one found in the friary at San Giovanni Rotondo, often made use of by St. Padre Pio, should have a place in our homes. Located on a landing in the cloister is a list of one hundred sins, many of which souls in purgation suffer to be cleansed of, titled 'A Short and Easy Way to Pray for the Holy Souls in Purgatory.' This is a box containing numbered disks corresponding to the list of sins. Padre Pio would, when passing by, select a disk and recite an 'Eternal Rest' for those souls being purged of the indicated sin. Then, much happier, he would proceed on his painful way" — Father Alessio Parente, O.F.M. Cap., promoter of the teachings of St. Pio of Pietrelcina.

Reflection: Make a "purgatory box" for the family.

---

*Eternal rest grant unto them, O Lord, and let perpetual
light shine upon them. May they rest in peace. Amen.*

Mary's Messengers of Love

"But a Samaritan, as he journeyed, came to where he was; and when he saw him, he had compassion, and went to him and bound up all his wounds, pouring on oil and wine; then he set him on his own beast and brought him to an inn, and took care of him." — Luke 10:33-34

"Let us be zealous in this practice of gaining indulgences. Let us think of those whom we have placed in purgatory. Let us animate ourselves, when weary, by the thought of those patient, peaceful sufferers; let us be good Samaritans to those suffering souls; let us bring them relief; let us lessen their pains by administering the healing balsam of the Precious Blood. We can ourselves administer it. We can be Mary's messengers of love to her imprisoned children" — Mother Mary Potter, foundress of the Little Company of Mary Sisters, author.

Reflection: A very powerful way to pray for the holy souls is to enlist the help of our Blessed Mother, asking her to pour the Precious Blood upon them. God has put the Precious Blood and its saving power at Our Lady's disposal, to dispense as she sees fit.

Eternal rest grant unto them, O Lord, and let perpetual light shine upon them. May they rest in peace. Amen.

Little Compacts

"Accept, I pray you, my gift that is brought to you, because God has dealt graciously with me, and because I have enough." — *Genesis 33:11*

St. Catherine of Bologna had a most tender devotion toward the holy souls in purgatory. She prayed for them frequently and with the greatest fervor. She recommended herself to them with the greatest confidence in her spiritual necessities and advised others to do the same, saying: "When I wish to obtain any favor from our Father in Heaven, I have recourse to the souls that are detained in purgatory. I entreat them to present my request to the Divine Majesty in their own name, and I feel that I am heard through their intercession."

Reflection: Submit yourself to the influence of the holy souls to avoid purgatory.

Eternal rest grant unto them, O Lord, and let perpetual light shine upon them. May they rest in peace. Amen.

A Circle of Prayer

"O Lord, God of Israel, there is no God like thee, in heaven above or on earth beneath, keeping covenant and showing steadfast love to thy servants who walk before thee with all their heart." — 1 Kings 8:23

"Oh! If it were but known how great is the power of the good souls in purgatory with the Heart of God, and if we knew all the graces we can obtain through their intercession, they would not be so much forgotten. We must, therefore, pray much for them, that they may pray much for us" — St. John Vianney.

Reflection: Come full circle. End your evening in prayer remembering the poor souls. They are really *poor souls* because they are soon forgotten. The blessed souls invest so much hope in our prayers.

Eternal rest grant unto them, O Lord, and let perpetual light shine upon them. May they rest in peace. Amen.

JULY 14

The Liberator

*I stretch out my hands to thee; my soul thirsts for
thee like a parched land. — Psalm 143:6*

St. Nicholas of Tolentino is the patron of the holy souls. He saw a great
number of suffering souls of every age and condition in a field begging
him to celebrate Holy Mass for them. The holy priest wept. After offering
Mass for eight days, all the souls he had seen were released.

Reflection: Become a liberator for the souls in purgatory. If one person can liberate our friends, think what the thousands of us can do.
The souls never forget their friends!

---

*Eternal rest grant unto them, O Lord, and let perpetual
light shine upon them. May they rest in peace. Amen.*

Healing and Eternal Love

May the God of peace himself sanctify you wholly; and may your spirit and soul and body be kept sound and blameless at the coming of our Lord Jesus Christ. — 1 Thessalonians 5:23

When St. Thérèse of Lisieux was suffering from excessive scrupulosity and nothing seemed to be helping, she decided to ask her deceased brothers and sisters to win for her the grace of healing. She wanted them to "show me that in heaven they still knew how to love! The answer was not long in coming, for soon peace came to inundate my soul with its delightful waves, and I knew then that if I was loved on earth, I was also loved in heaven. Since that moment, my devotion for my little brothers and sisters has grown and I love to hold dialogues with them frequently, to speak with them about the sadness of our exile, my desire to join them soon in the Fatherland!"

Reflection: Do what the Holy Spirit inspires you to do for the holy souls.

Eternal rest grant unto them, O Lord, and let perpetual light shine upon them. May they rest in peace. Amen.

JULY 16

The Sabbatine Privilege

For thou hast delivered my soul from death, yea, my feet from falling,
that I may walk before God in the light of life. — *Psalm 56:13*

"Our Lady has promised that those who wear the Scapular of Mount Carmel (the Brown Scapular) are released from purgatory on the first Saturday after their death, fulfilling all the duties required (observe chastity according to one's state in life, pray the daily Rosary). We recall that Père Lamy, who saw the coming triumph of the Immaculate Heart of Mary said: 'As for Our Lady, her kindness, gets her everywhere.... A soul that is falling into hell and calls on her is helped. The Blessed Virgin said again to me one day that those who have fulfilled the conditions of her Sabbatine Privilege (the above duties and wearing the scapular) will be drawn out of purgatory by her on the first Saturday after death'" — International Pilgrim Virgin Statue Foundation.

Reflection: Promote and wear the Brown Scapular.

Eternal rest grant unto them, O Lord, and let perpetual
light shine upon them. May they rest in peace. Amen.

Be Serious about Your Spiritual Life

And I said: "Woe is me! For I am lost; for I am a man of unclean lips, and I dwell in the midst of a people of unclean lips; for my eyes have seen the King, the LORD of hosts!" Then flew one of the seraphim to me, having in his hand a burning coal which he had taken with tongs from the altar. And he touched my mouth, and said: "Behold, this has touched your lips; your guilt is taken away, and your sin forgiven." — Isaiah 6:5-7

"The same fire burns the lost ... and the saved" — St. Augustine.

Reflection: Pray for the conversion of those still here on earth who have greatly sinned and who have let evil rule their lives. Pray that they convert while there is still time for them to make it to purgatory. Offer a Mass for the conversion of sinners. Who hurt you? Who are your enemies? Offer a Mass for them, too.

Eternal rest grant unto them, O Lord, and let perpetual light shine upon them. May they rest in peace. Amen.

Be Prepared

Go to the ant, O sluggard; consider her ways, and be wise. Without having any chief, officer or ruler, she prepares her food in summer, and gathers her sustenance in harvest. — Proverbs 6:6-8

"In his play *Hamlet*, William Shakespeare demonstrated his understanding of the piteous plight of the poor purgatorial soul and its sufferings, when the Ghost of Hamlet's father says:

Cut off even in the blossoms of my sin,
Unhousel'd, disappointed, unaneral'd;
No reckoning made, but sent to my account
With all my imperfections on my head.
O horrible! O horrible! Most horrible!

"In terms of Shakespeare's *Hamlet*, 'unhousel'd' means 'without the holy Eucharist.' 'Unaneral'd' indicates that a person has not received the Sacrament of the Sick. 'No reckoning made' is Shakespeare's way of saying that a man is unconfessed, sent to his account un-absolved of his sins, with all his imperfections on his head. What a pregnant phrase! No wonder *Hamlet* bewails this state as 'Horrible! Most horrible!' " — Father Scott Haynes, S.J.C., author.

Reflection: To die a "happy death" is not to die in the state in which we live but in the "state of grace." We must petition God for this grace throughout life. Offer a Mass for this intention.

Eternal rest grant unto them, O Lord, and let perpetual light shine upon them. May they rest in peace. Amen.

Angelic Reminders

*"See that you do not despise one of these little ones; for I
tell you that in heaven their angels always behold the face
of my Father who is in heaven." — Matthew 18:10*

"It is probable that the holy angels are the sources from whom proceed a thousand suggestions to us to pray for the holy souls, sudden remembrances of them, feelings as if they were near and in need of our prayers" — St. Gregory.

Reflection: Each one of us has an angel at our side as instructor and guide, directing our life. Do not take these pure blessed spirits for granted. Throughout this day, pray: "Holy angel, my light, enlighten me."

---

*Eternal rest grant unto them, O Lord, and let perpetual
light shine upon them. May they rest in peace. Amen.*

Comfort for the Lord

*"The Spirit of the Lord is upon me, because he has anointed
me to preach good news to the poor. He has sent me to proclaim
release to the captives and recovering of sight to the blind,
to set at liberty those who are oppressed." — Luke 4:18*

"He [God] is greatly satisfied when, through our prayers, a soul is released
from purgatory. It is as if we had released the Lord Himself from prison"
— St. Gertrude.

Reflection: Readily forgive all injuries. Offer this act of virtue for
Jesus' saintly souls who are so dear to Him.

---

*Eternal rest grant unto them, O Lord, and let perpetual
light shine upon them. May they rest in peace. Amen.*

JULY 21

Come, Holy Spirit!

"The wind blows where it wills, and you hear the sound of it,
but you do not know whence it comes or whither it goes; so it
is with every one who is born of the Spirit." — John 3:8

"Constant, generous love for the holy souls, love whose secret life-breath is prayer and sacrifice on their behalf, is a great gift of the Holy Spirit. It is an infusion of his love into the soul whom he desires to be the vehicle of his mercies to the souls in purgatory. This infusion of love, always singular in its kind, gives the recipient a corresponding distinctive beauty of love for the pain-stricken multitudes of purgatory even as it gives him a singular love for God. For love of God and our neighbor will ever be inseparable. All ends in the love of God"— Father Hubert, O.F.M. Cap., author.

Reflection: As a flaming joy, the Holy Spirit enkindles love for these afflicted ones in whom, when, where, in what manner and in what measure He pleases. But we must be open to His inspirations.

Eternal rest grant unto them, O Lord, and let perpetual
light shine upon them. May they rest in peace. Amen.

Dare to Believe

*For we are his workmanship, created in Christ Jesus
for good works, which God prepared beforehand, that
we should walk in them.* — *Ephesians 2:10*

"Remember always the dear departed through our prayers and good works, and we should also do many good works for the benefit of our own souls while we have the chance in this life. We should pay no attention to those who scoff or laugh at us, say that purgatory does not exist. Perhaps they even dare to say that it is in our imagination. If it is in our imagination, then it is also in the imaginations of all those saints who have gone before us and who have left their testimony behind them" — Thomas à Kempis, German Canon Regular, author.

Reflection: Do not be disturbed if your good works are criticized. Take this as a trial of purity of intention.

---

*Eternal rest grant unto them, O Lord, and let perpetual
light shine upon them. May they rest in peace. Amen.*

Friends of the Living

*As the eyes of servants look to the hand of their master, as the
eyes of a maid to the hand of her mistress, so our eyes look to the
LORD our God, till he have mercy upon us. — Psalm 123:2*

St. Bridget heard the souls in purgatory call to heaven, saying in a loud
voice: "O merciful God, reward a hundredfold the charity of them that by
their good works assist us to come from out of this darkness to the eternal
light and to attain your Beatific Vision."

Reflection: Who did you the most good spiritually? Financially?
Give them the joy of a Holy Mass. Show your gratitude, a virtue
that's a part of justice. It pleases God and gains for us great merit.

---

*Eternal rest grant unto them, O Lord, and let perpetual
light shine upon them. May they rest in peace. Amen.*

Dante on the Soul's Journey

Who shall ascend the hill of the LORD? And who shall stand in his holy place? He who has clean hands and a pure heart, who does not lift up his soul to what is false, and does not swear deceitfully. He will receive blessing from the LORD, and vindication from the God of his salvation. Such is the generation of those who seek him, who seek the face of the God of Jacob. — Psalm 24:3-6

In his *Divine Comedy*, the poet Dante has Virgil say: "This mountain's of such sort that climbing it is hardest at the start; but as we rise, the slope seems to you so gentle that climbing farther up will be as restful as traveling downstream by boat, you will be where this pathway ends, and there you can expect to put your weariness to rest" (*Purgatorio*, Canto 4).

"The closer a soul is to the bottom of the mountain, the harder it is to motivate himself to climb upwards, partly because the path is so steep. As he purges himself of his sins, though, his suffering eases and he actually feels lighter as he climbs higher. The higher he climbs, the easier the path becomes, so that his virtue increases along with his willingness to suffer as he climbs" — Allen Mandelbaum, American professor of Italian literature, poet, translator of the *Divine Comedy*.

Reflection: Pray: "Almighty God, help me in these fleeting days that I may not use my time to consider and hesitate, but be positive in my desires and pursue them. Grant me strength to hold each day precious, and live it more than consistently."

Eternal rest grant unto them, O Lord, and let perpetual light shine upon them. May they rest in peace. Amen.

The Slothful's Haste

Through sloth the roof sinks in, and through indolence
the house leaks. — Ecclesiastes 10:18

"Following them, the others [the Slothful] cried: 'Quick, quick, lest time be lost through insufficient love; where urge for good is keen, grace finds new green" — Dante (*Purgatorio*, Canto 18).

"The Slothful are punished by an immoderate sense of haste; they feel the urge to rush everywhere. This obviously has physical ramifications, wearing down their bodies and feet, but also not allowing their minds to reflect and relax. However, the sense of justice pervades here — as with all the penitents — because 'where urge for good is keen,' 'grace finds new green.' They realize that their suffering now will result in a rebirth ('new green') of their grace, after which they'll be permitted to enter Heaven" — Allen Mandelbaum, American professor of Italian literature, poet, translator of the *Divine Comedy*.

Reflection: Slow down, pause, and reflect. Pray for those who sinned the most because of laziness.

Eternal rest grant unto them, O Lord, and let perpetual
light shine upon them. May they rest in peace. Amen.

The Vice of Envy

Let us have no self-conceit, no provoking of one another,
no envy of one another. — Galatians 5:26

In his *Divine Comedy*, the poet Dante has the nobleman Guido del Duca say: "My blood was so afire with envy that, when I had seen a man becoming happy, the lividness in me was plain to see. From what I've sown, this is the straw I reap: O humankind, why do you set your hearts there where our sharing cannot have a part?" (*Purgatorio*, Canto 14).

"Guido admits that the vice of envy includes more than just jealously wanting someone else's belongings; it also includes wishing ill on that other person simply because he has something that the envious lacks. Guido's 'lividness' here is a testament to the rage he felt against the person whom he envied. But, again, he justifies his punishment: 'From what I've sown, this is the straw I reap.' Of course, 'straw' is not very valuable, so Guido suggests that what he sewed in life was not something to be envied" — Allen Mandelbaum, American professor of Italian literature, poet, translator of the *Divine Comedy*.

Reflection: Dissolve envy. Pray for those who sinned the most because of envy.

Eternal rest grant unto them, O Lord, and let perpetual
light shine upon them. May they rest in peace. Amen.

The Cowardice of Mediocrity

And whatever you do, in word or deed, do everything
in the name of the Lord Jesus, giving thanks to God
the Father through him. — Colossians 3:17

"The mediocre person gives himself to God but reserves a certain part of his life for himself. He does not see all the consequences of a change in his life. He does not direct his whole will to respond to the call of God's grace, still giving in, in part, to evil tendencies. This is a decision for God, but with a request that God not take him seriously. It is a choice for Light, but with a lingering and morbid fascinations for darkness.

"These are situations we understand because we experience them every day. Our faith calls these small acts of cowardice venial sins. They lack the fullness of charity. We give something, but keep something back. We mount the cross, but only with one hand and one foot. What can be done, Lord, with people like us? With useless servants like this? Are there many, perhaps all of us?" — Father Stephen Torraco, Regina Coeli Academy.

Reflection: Dear Lord, help us to be utterly grateful for your unfathomable mystery of purgatory. Pray an Act of Faith: "O my God, I firmly believe that you are one God in three divine Persons, Father, Son, and Holy Spirit. I believe that your divine Son became man and died for our sins, and that he will come to judge the living and the dead. I believe these and all the truths which the holy Catholic Church teaches, because you have revealed them, who can neither deceive nor be deceived. Amen."

Eternal rest grant unto them, O Lord, and let perpetual
light shine upon them. May they rest in peace. Amen.

Jesus' Pledge to You

Do not be conformed to this world but be transformed by the renewing of your mind, so that you may prove what is the will of God, what is good and acceptable and perfect. — Romans 12:2

" 'Make no mistake,' He [Jesus] says, 'if you let Me I will make you perfect. The moment you put yourself in My hands, that is what you are in for. Nothing less, or other than that. You have free will, and if you choose, you can push Me away. But if you do not push Me away, understand that I am going to see this job through. Whatever suffering it may cost you after death, whatever it costs Me, I will never rest, nor let you rest, until you are literally perfect — until My Father can say without reservation that He is well pleased with you, as He said He was well pleased with Me. This I can do and will do. But, I will not do anything less' " — C. S. Lewis, lay theologian, Christian apologist, poet, author.

Reflection: Do ordinary things well.

Eternal rest grant unto them, O Lord, and let perpetual light shine upon them. May they rest in peace. Amen.

Saintly Sufferers

*We are afflicted in every way, but not crushed; perplexed but not driven
to despair; persecuted, but not forsaken; struck down, but not destroyed;
always carrying in the body the death of Jesus, so that the life of Jesus
may also be manifested in our bodies. — 2 Corinthians 4:8-10*

Imagine the gates of purgatory wide open with no guards to prevent possible escape from that terrible prison. But you would never see any of the
holy souls even try to slip away.

In the words of author C. S. Lewis, "Our souls demand purgatory,
don't they? Would it not break the heart if God said to us, 'It is true, my
son, that your breath smells and your rags drip with mud and slime, but
we are charitable here and no one will upbraid you with these things, nor
draw away from you. Enter into the joy'? Should we not reply, 'With sub-
mission, sir, and if there is no objection, I'd rather be cleaned first.' 'It may
hurt, you know.' 'Even so, sir.'"

Reflection: Pray with Blessed Cardinal John Henry Newman:
"Jesus, spare these souls which are so dear to you, souls who in
prison [purgatory], calm and patient, wait for you; hasten, Lord,
their hour, and bid them come to you, to that glorious home, where
they shall ever gaze on you."

---

*Eternal rest grant unto them, O Lord, and let perpetual
light shine upon them. May they rest in peace. Amen.*

God Is Their Rest and Peace

*My people will abide in a peaceful habitation, in secure
dwellings, and in quiet resting places.* — Isaiah 32:18

"Since the holy souls possess through perfect charity the tranquility of
order — the order of perfect union with the divine will — they are in profound peace. Their happiness never fails; rather it increases as the time of
their exile draws to a close. That is why the Church refers to her departed
children as resting 'in the sleep of peace'" — Father Hubert, O.F.M.
Cap., author.

Reflection: "O holy souls on earth and in purgatory! What has God
not bestowed on us? Yea, God is ours as the Fount of Unselfish-
ness; Christ is ours as God Incarnate; Mary is ours as selflessness
immaculate; for love proceeds from God and cannot rest but in
God" — Thomas à Kempis, German Canon Regular, author.

---

*Eternal rest grant unto them, O Lord, and let perpetual
light shine upon them. May they rest in peace. Amen.*

They Hardly Ever Fail

*"The Lord God is watching over us and in truth has compassion
on us, as Moses declared in his song which bore witness
against the people to their faces, when he said, 'And he will
have compassion on his servants.'"* — *2 Maccabees 7:6*

The poor souls were the objects of many of Venerable Solanus Casey's prayers and devotions. Brother Ignatius noted: "His concern for the souls in purgatory was very evident in the many letters that he wrote to people which I have read and studied quite thoroughly. This was something he would recommend in the event that someone was asking for a favor, that they should pray for the poor souls in purgatory. In his mind, the poor souls, 'hardly ever fail.'"

Reflection: Father Solanus recommends that one should "make a promise" to the holy souls for a special intention. Let us do so, always accepting God's designs in all things.

---

*Eternal rest grant unto them, O Lord, and let perpetual
light shine upon them. May they rest in peace. Amen.*

AUGUST 1

A God of Infinite Mercy

So the Lord heard their prayers and looked upon their affliction;
for the people fasted many days throughout Judea and in Jerusalem
before the sanctuary of the Lord Almighty. — Judith 4:13

"Too strong an emphasis on purgatory as punishment is perhaps the wrong way to look at it. God is not trying to 'get even' with people, nor is purgatory his way of lowering the boom. In its deepest meaning the doctrine says that God is mercifully preparing unprepared creatures for the joys of heaven. They were charged by the gospel to prepare for heaven while alive on earth. He extended graces to help them prepare for these joys countless times. If people gave small notice to him and prepared much less seriously than they should have, do they not thereby find themselves at death in an uncertain and precarious position? Whose fault is that?" — Father Michael J. Taylor, S.J., Scripture scholar, author.

Reflection: Dear God, You allow me to make up for my faults and complete the mission You gave me on earth. Guide me as to how I can better prepare for life eternal.

Eternal rest grant unto them, O Lord, and let perpetual
light shine upon them. May they rest in peace. Amen.

Meeting Love

See what love the Father has given us, that we should be
called children of God; and so we are. — *1 John 3:1*

"To whatever extent we become conscious, during our earthly lives, of our inability to rid ourselves completely of whatever blocks us from intimate union with God, we feel [spiritual] pain. We experience a taste of 'purgatory,' recognizing how perfectly God loves us, and how imperfectly we love Him in return.... Purgatory is our meeting with Christ who loves us, and of our loving acceptance of His pardoning love. It is our passage to holiness" — Father Seraphim Michalenko, Marians of the Immaculate Conception, spreading the message of Divine Mercy for over fifty years.

Reflection: Sweet Jesus, liberate the souls who are so dear to You.

Eternal rest grant unto them, O Lord, and let perpetual
light shine upon them. May they rest in peace. Amen.

In Need of Curing

"He will wipe away every tear from their eyes, and death shall be no more, neither shall there be mourning nor crying nor pain anymore, for the former things have passed away." — Revelation 21:4

"She was a splendid thing, a soul straight, bright, and tempered like a sword. But not a perfected saint. A sinful woman married to a sinful man; two of God's patients not yet cured. I know there are not only tears to be dried but stains to be scoured. The sword will be made even brighter ... but, oh God, tenderly, tenderly" — C. S. Lewis, lay theologian, Christian apologist, poet, author.

Reflection: Acknowledge your deceased loved ones at weddings during the petitions at Mass.

Eternal rest grant unto them, O Lord, and let perpetual light shine upon them. May they rest in peace. Amen.

Mary's Sacrifice

But standing by the cross of Jesus were his mother and his mother's
sister, Mary the wife of Clopas, and Mary Magdalene. — *John 19:25*

Why does not Mary ask God to empty purgatory? A French Jesuit, Jean
Baptist Terrien, gives insight into this question. He explains that the mercy
of Mary would be marked by wisdom. In God's wisdom, Mary does not
fix every problem, both here on earth and in the case of the Church Suffering in purgatory.

He writes: "Mary understands both justice and love to a degree no
other human person can because of her unique participation in our
redemption." In St. John Paul II's encyclical *Rich in Mercy*: "No one has
experienced, to the same degree as the Mother of the crucified One, the
mystery of the cross, the overwhelming encounter of divine transcendent
justice with love: that 'kiss' given by mercy to justice. No one has received
into his heart, as much as Mary did, that mystery, that truly divine dimen-
sion of the redemption effected on Calvary by means of the death of the
Son, together with the sacrifice of her maternal heart, together with her
definitive 'fiat.'"

Reflection: Let us remember that those who have gone before us
have not automatically entered heaven. Therefore, pray on behalf
of the suffering soul who most needs God's mercy.

Eternal rest grant unto them, O Lord, and let perpetual
light shine upon them. May they rest in peace. Amen.

Mother Mary Intercedes for Us

"For he who is mighty has done great things for me." — Luke 1:49

"The Blessed Virgin offers our prayers to God. She embellishes them.... Divinely skillful, she knows how to make gold of our dross.... The prayer, even when made with little attention is always a prayer, and our Blessed Mother supplies that which lacks.... She is ceaselessly busy in covering our weaknesses before the face of God. We feel her bounty, her charity. If she showed severity, we would be immediately overwhelmed; we would disappear from before the face of God" — Père Jean Édouard Lamy, mystic, founder of the Religious Congregation of the Servants of Jesus and Mary, author.

Reflection: Let Mary take over. Give her everything.

Eternal rest grant unto them, O Lord, and let perpetual light shine upon them. May they rest in peace. Amen.

AUGUST 6

God's Justice

*"Your prayers and your alms have ascended
as a memorial before God." — Acts 10:4*

St. Bridget had multiple experiences of purgatory. Once she saw a soul suffering there in a way like gold is purified in a crucible. She heard an angel say, "Blessed be the mortal that hastens to the relief of the suffering souls."

The justice of God demands that the holy souls either be purified in the flames of purgatory or be released from there by the good deeds of their friends.

Reflection: Perform "little errands" for the sick and the elderly, small and hidden acts only God sees, done with tender love of the grateful souls.

---

*Eternal rest grant unto them, O Lord, and let perpetual
light shine upon them. May they rest in peace. Amen.*

AUGUST 7

Longing for Salvation

*"Repent and be baptized every one of you in the name of
Jesus Christ for the forgiveness of your sins; and you shall
receive the gift of the Holy Spirit." — Acts 2:38*

"The one who is animated by a longing for personal salvation and the
salvation of others is helping the souls in purgatory. It is quite obvious: if
someone treats lightly his own salvation, his friendship with the Lord, he
won't be concerned with the fate of the other people on earth, and even
less about those in purgatory. Such can be a lukewarm Christian, with
a cold and egotistical heart" — Father Janusz Kumala, Marians of the
Immaculate Conception.

Reflection: Do not wait until the last hour to seek reconciliation
with God and neighbor. You may not be here next year. Prepare
daily for eternal life with an attitude of forgiveness and actions.

---

*Eternal rest grant unto them, O Lord, and let perpetual
light shine upon them. May they rest in peace. Amen.*

A Necessary Purification

And he came to her and said, "Hail full of grace,
the Lord is with you!" — Luke 1:28

A young girl who had been released from purgatory by the prayers of St. Dominic appeared to him and said: "In the name of the souls in purgatory, I invoke you to preach throughout the whole world devotion to the holy Rosary, and urge the faithful to apply to those souls the indulgences attached to it. The Blessed Virgin and the angels rejoice at this devotion, and the souls set free will pray in heaven for their deliverers."

Reflection: Urge another to join in praying the Rosary for the holy souls. It is the most powerful Marian prayer on earth.

Eternal rest grant unto them, O Lord, and let perpetual
light shine upon them. May they rest in peace. Amen.

Why Should We Lament?

For my angel is with you, and he is watching your lives. — *Baruch 6:7*

"Our dead are not as far as we think. Without seeing them, we can converse with them and share our feelings with them. If they are in heaven, faith tells us that they still care for us, and in God see what we are doing and hear the words we tell them and that they pray for us. If they are in purgatory, it is easy to entrust to our guardian angel the messages we want to send them. Why should we not imitate that pious daughter, St. Mary Magdalen de Pazzi, who, having lost her mother, never ceased to converse with her through her good angel? She told her all her difficulties, and asked her advice.

"Whatever light and consolation she received, she attributed it to that loving mother" — St. Peter Faure.

Reflection: Intercede for your deceased loved ones through your guardian angel. Ask that the holy souls find relief and release.

Eternal rest grant unto them, O Lord, and let perpetual light shine upon them. May they rest in peace. Amen.

Yearning for God

I adjure you, O daughters of Jerusalem, if you find my beloved,
that you tell him I am sick with love. — Song of Solomon 5:8

"The essence of the pains of purgatory is the love which souls have for God — love which is continually increased by their more perfect knowledge of His perfections, and is manifested by the intensity of their desire to behold and possess Him. It is a hunger, a thirst, a fever for God. This desire borrows something from the sovereign greatness of its object. The intensity of the longing is indescribable; their whole being is merged and concentrated in it" — Father Martin Jugie, Assumptionist, Byzantine scholar, author.

Reflection: Imagine your greatest love and longing and know that it cannot compare to that of the holy souls as they await being brought into the presence of the Lord.

Eternal rest grant unto them, O Lord, and let perpetual
light shine upon them. May they rest in peace. Amen.

AUGUST 11

Authentic Creatures

*I consider that the sufferings of this present time are not worth
comparing with the glory that is to be revealed to us.* — Romans 8:18

In his *Dark Night of the Soul*, St. John of the Cross tells us: "For this purgation is what would have to be undergone there. The soul that endures it
here on earth either does not enter that place, or is detained there for only
a short while. It gains more in one hour here on earth by this purgation
than it would in many there."

Reflection: There is no escape from the purification we need, but
our efforts while still on our earthly pilgrimage are most valuable.
What needs to be purged from our lives now to more quickly gain
release from purgatory when the time comes?

---

*Eternal rest grant unto them, O Lord, and let perpetual
light shine upon them. May they rest in peace. Amen.*

Be a Blessing

Do not appear before the Lord empty-handed, for all these things
are to be done because of the commandment. — *Sirach 35:4-5*

"The sooner the purification happens, and the more advanced it can become, the better for us and everyone else. The more we are purified and conformed to God's will the happier we will be, better able to love God, those around us and be a blessing for others in our life. St. John explains that the degree of this purification depends on how much one needs to be purified and to what degree of union God is leading the person" — Ralph Martin, president of Renewal Ministries, professor, author.

Reflection: Jesus emptied Himself, taking the form of a servant. May we empty ourselves of self-love and take up a life lived in love of others.

Eternal rest grant unto them, O Lord, and let perpetual
light shine upon them. May they rest in peace. Amen.

Perpetual Light

"Behold, I make all things new." — Revelation 21:5

"We do not know how long some souls are detained in purgatory, but we do know that when they emerge from the darkness into the light of God's presence, they are perfect. Every angle is perfect. Every facet is clear, like cut and mounted diamonds. The dazzling beam of God's light renders them incandescent without causing pain, resistance, or distortion. His light now lights up the thousand angles of their rich characters developed via life's experiences. The wealth of their talents reflects his light into brilliant rainbow colors. The saints are all lovely in their beauty. Swept up by the Spirit, they flow with elation in the stream of God's love for himself. Like Moses, they jubilate in the endless wealth of the I AM, of God's boundless love, truth, and beauty, of essential Splendor pulsing with life" — Father Anthony Zimmerman, professor emeritus of moral theology, Nanzan University in Aagoya, Japan.

Reflection: Pray before the Blessed Sacrament for the detained souls. Blessed Paul VI wrote: "To visit the Blessed Sacrament is ... a proof of gratitude, and expression of love, and a duty of adoration toward Christ our Lord."

Eternal rest grant unto them, O Lord, and let perpetual light shine upon them. May they rest in peace. Amen.

Mercy on Yourselves

A man who is kind benefits himself. — Proverbs 11:17

"A wealthy Genoese merchant when he died left no provisions for suffrages for his soul. Everyone wondered why a man who had been so devout and charitable to others did not include Masses in his will. A notebook was found. Over 2,000 Masses were celebrated for others which he personally attended. At the end of the notebook was written: 'Let anyone who wishes to be certain of having good done to him procure it himself during his lifetime'" — St. Leonard of Port Maurice.

Reflection: Give the gift of Masses for all occasions.

Eternal rest grant unto them, O Lord, and let perpetual light shine upon them. May they rest in peace. Amen.

AUGUST 15

Be Free

For you had compassion on the prisoners. — Hebrews 10:34

"At the time of Mary's Assumption, all of purgatory was emptied, and the souls detained there accompanied her in her triumphant entry into heaven. From that time on the Blessed Virgin has enjoyed the privilege of freeing her servants from those pains" — St. Peter Damian.

Reflection: The great saints assert that devotion to Our Lady is a sign of predestination, as well as lessening our own purgatorial pains and the souls to whom we practice this devotion. Enroll your loved ones in one of the many Marian association memberships. (See page 395 for more information.)

Eternal rest grant unto them, O Lord, and let perpetual light shine upon them. May they rest in peace. Amen.

AUGUST 16

Protection under the Mother of Mercy

"Do whatever he tells you." — John 2:5

"A great servant of Mary, Blessed Renier of Citeaux, trembled at the thought of his sins and the terrible Justice of God after death. In his fear, addressing himself to his great Protectress, who calls herself Mother of Mercy, he was rapt in spirit and saw the Mother of God supplicating her son in his favor. 'My Son,' she said, 'deal mercifully with him in purgatory, because he humbly repents of his sins.' 'My Mother,' replied Jesus, 'I place his cause in your hands,' which meant to say, be it done to your client according to your desire. Blessed Renier understood with unutterable joy that Mary had obtained his exemption from purgatory" — Father F. X. Schouppe, S.J., author.

Reflection: Make some small donation to a group whose ministry involves the holy souls.

Eternal rest grant unto them, O Lord, and let perpetual light shine upon them. May they rest in peace. Amen.

God Is Who Is

"You are dust, and to dust you shall return." — Genesis 3:19

"God defined Himself to Moses: 'I AM WHO I AM' (Exodus 3:14). He defined human nature to St. Catherine of Siena when He said: 'I am Who am — thou art, who are not.'

"After the souls in purgatory have seen the darkness of sin in the Light of God, their ingratitude in His Long-suffering, their latent imperfections in His Sanctity, the knowledge must go deeper still and sound their nothingness and emptiness in the plentitude of His Self-existence. They must feel to the depth that 'They are who are not' before Him 'Who is'" — Mother Mary of St. Austin, Helpers of the Holy Souls, author.

Reflection: Pray for all souls in your family — past, present, and future — until the end of time.

Eternal rest grant unto them, O Lord, and let perpetual light shine upon them. May they rest in peace. Amen.

I Thirst

And the blood of Jesus his Son cleanses us from all sin. — *1 John 1:7*

"Blessed Henry Suso, the Dominican, when studying at Cologne, had a great friend belonging to the same Order. When they parted, after finishing their studies, they agreed that whichever of the two should survive the other should say two Masses for his deceased friend every week. The friend died first, but Suso forgot his promise to say the Masses, and contented himself with prayers for his soul. One day, when at prayer he heard a noise behind him. He took no notice at first, and continued his prayers. After a time, however, he heard a voice, which he recognized as his deceased friend, reproaching him for his forgetfulness. He excused himself by saying that he had often prayed for him, but his friend replied: 'I need Blood to quench the flames by which I am tormented — the Blood of Jesus Christ, offered in the Holy Sacrifice of the Mass.' Suso remembered his promise, and every week afterwards offered the Mass for his friend's soul. Some time afterwards his friend appeared to him again, and thanked him for his charity, which had released him from purgatory" — *Life of Blessed Henry Suso* (Thomas Francis Knox, translator).

Reflection: Pray or sing: "O Sacrament Most Holy, O Sacrament Divine, all praise and all thanksgiving be every moment Thine."

Eternal rest grant unto them, O Lord, and let perpetual light shine upon them. May they rest in peace. Amen.

Enduring Suffering

"If any man would come after me, let him deny himself and take up his cross and follow me. For whoever would save his life will lose it, and whoever loses his life for my sake will find it." — *Matthew 16:24*

"Suddenly I saw the complete condition of my soul as God sees it. I could clearly see all that is displeasing to God. I did not know that even the smallest transgressions will have to be accounted for. What a moment! Who can describe it? To stand before the Thrice-Holy God! Jesus asked me, Who are you? I answered 'I am your servant, Lord.' You are guilty of one day of fire in purgatory. I wanted to throw myself immediately into the flames of purgatory, but Jesus stopped me and said, Which do you prefer, suffer now for one day in purgatory or for a short while on earth? I replied, 'Jesus, I want to suffer in purgatory, and I want to suffer also the greatest pains on earth, even if it were to the end of the world.' Jesus said, One [of the two] is enough; you will go back to earth, and there you will suffer much, but not for long; you will accomplish My will and My desires, and a faithful servant of Mine will help you do this. Now rest your head on My bosom, on My heart, and draw from it strength and power for these sufferings because you will find neither relief nor help nor comfort anywhere else. Know that you will have much, much to suffer, but don't let this frighten you; I am with you" — St. Faustina (*Diary*, 36).

Reflection: The departed souls "rest in peace." Peacefully endure all trials.

Eternal rest grant unto them, O Lord, and let perpetual light shine upon them. May they rest in peace. Amen.

Light of the Soul

"For I know the plans I have for you, says the Lord, plans for welfare and not for evil, to give you a future and a hope." — Jeremiah 29:11

"We are given this light at death to see the plan God has had for us from the beginning. We then understand how we have chosen to comply with His Divine Plan. In the light of truth, we know where we belong, where we fit, and we choose heaven, hell, or purgatory" — St. Catherine of Siena.

Reflection: Surrender your own plan to God's divine plan. You have been chosen by God in His great plan of salvation.

Eternal rest grant unto them, O Lord, and let perpetual light shine upon them. May they rest in peace. Amen.

Mother of the Church Suffering

And Melchizedek king of Salem brought out bread and wine;
he was priest of God Most High. — Genesis 14:18

Archdeacon Bartholomew Cavanagh was pastor of the parish in Knock, Ireland, where Our Lady appeared on the gable of the church in 1879. He had a great devotion to the souls in purgatory. Months before the apparition, the archdeacon offered one hundred Masses for the souls in purgatory. It was on the hundredth day that Mass was offered that Our Lady appeared in Knock, on August 21, 1879, as a gift of gratitude of the released souls.

Reflection: Get some friends together and offer one hundred Masses for the souls in purgatory and for world peace.

Eternal rest grant unto them, O Lord, and let perpetual
light shine upon them. May they rest in peace. Amen.

Charitable Suffering

*If you pour yourself out for the hungry and satisfy the desire
of the afflicted, then shall your light rise in the darkness
and your gloom be as the noonday. — Isaiah 58:10*

"The gift that a man makes of his good works and indulgences in favor of the souls in purgatory, far from diminishing his merits, multiplies them a hundredfold in the sight of God. When a man suffers for another for charity's sake, the satisfaction or the penance that he offers is more pleasing to God than if he offered it for Himself" — St. Thomas Aquinas (*Contra Gentiles,* Book II).

Reflection: Review your deceased family and friends. Who most needs your sacrifices on their behalf? Do not delay in offering charitable deeds for them today.

---

*Eternal rest grant unto them, O Lord, and let perpetual
light shine upon them. May they rest in peace. Amen.*

Agony of Love

*We know that the whole creation has been groaning
in travail together until now. — Romans 8:22*

"Reflect on the nature of the soul. Consider, on the one hand, its vast capacities, its unbounded powers of love, its everlasting life, its endless yearnings, its insatiable thirst, which creatures can indeed provoke, but never appease. On the other hand, contemplate God; His infinite beauty; His uncreated loveliness; His eternal truth; Him for whom alone the soul is made; who alone can fill it, satisfy it, and inundate it; and then judge of the agony it must suffer if hindered in its search after Him" — Monsignor John S. Vaughan, Irish author.

Reflection: Contemplate some of the many dimensions of God's infinite love for all His beloved souls.

---

*Eternal rest grant unto them, O Lord, and let perpetual
light shine upon them. May they rest in peace. Amen.*

The Advice of Angels

The angel of the LORD encamps around those who
fear him and delivers them. — Psalm 34:7

Sister Marie Denise de Martignat, of the Order of the Visitation, who died in the odor of sanctity, used to confide to the guardian angels of the souls in purgatory the prayers she offered for them and the messages she wished to send them. The charitable nun felt she was surrounded by those good protecting angels, who made known to her the necessities of the suffering souls committed to their charge, and showed her what she was to do for their deliverance.

Reflection: Ask your guardian angel to inspire you to know what is most needed by the holy souls.

Eternal rest grant unto them, O Lord, and let perpetual
light shine upon them. May they rest in peace. Amen.

First Holy Mass

[T]hat he might become a merciful and faithful high priest in the service of God, to make expiation for the sins of the people. — Hebrews 2:17

"A holy man whom God permitted to see the flames of purgatory recognized in the midst of them one of his friends, who showed extraordinary joy; and on being asked the reason, replied: 'My guardian angel has just told me of the birth of a child who will one day become a priest, and obtain my release from this place of pain by the first Mass he celebrates'" — Bishop Fernando Correia de Lacerda, seventeenth-century Portuguese prelate.

Reflection: Pray and offer sacrifices for those being called to the priesthood.

Eternal rest grant unto them, O Lord, and let perpetual light shine upon them. May they rest in peace. Amen.

The Rust of Sin

I appeal to you therefore, brethren, by the mercies of God, to present your bodies as a living sacrifice, holy and acceptable to God, which is your spiritual worship. — Romans 12:1

"St. Catherine of Genoa depicts purgatory as a process through which the effects of sin — referred to as the 'rust of sin' — are purged away. It is the infusion of this fiery love of God into the soul — so attractive, yet, at the same time, so painfully felt — which burns away the real substantive effects selfishness and other vices leave upon the soul. Scripture refers to these effects as blemishes, spots and defilements. We are called to be found without these effects when the Lord calls us to heaven. This implies one important truth: Christians are found with imperfections. We can purify these imperfections through faith, love, and sacrifice" — Abbé Cloquet, French author.

Reflection: Trim off common vices through faith, love, and sacrifice.

Eternal rest grant unto them, O Lord, and let perpetual light shine upon them. May they rest in peace. Amen.

Perfect Harmony

*And above all these put on love, which binds everything
together in perfect harmony. — Colossians 3:14*

"Suppose that some members of an orchestra executing a grand symphony
of a master composer take a few notes that do not accord with the right
order of the musical composition. These regrettable mistakes lessen the
perfection of the rendering as a whole.

"God is the master composer who has written the glorious symphony of
creation which he desires to be a perfect unity in the beauty of his own Spirit.
He has so sensitized the holy souls to their violations of that unity by their
unworthy 'moral attitudes' during their earthly life that they now experience
a mysterious agony of love for having disappointed Love by such behavior....

"The holy souls gladly endure the just 'repercussions' of that divine order
desired everywhere by God. To the now highly sensitized souls, these 'repercussions' of the world are so dynamic, painful, searing, as to issue a mysterious fire for them. A *fire of repentant love* all keen with pain, alive with
suffering of having introduced the ugliness of their own disorder into the
beauty of that order willed by God, for having opposed their own will to the
divine will" — Karl Rahner, S.J., German theologian, author.

Reflection: Holy souls, you who are so very near me, pray God to
engulf me in the transforming might of His love. Help me to emu-
late you by giving God the gracious hospitality of freedom in my
soul.

---

*Eternal rest grant unto them, O Lord, and let perpetual
light shine upon them. May they rest in peace. Amen.*

AUGUST 28

Salvation with the Souls

"If you ask anything in my name, I will do it." — *John 14:14*

"He who assists these distressed souls, so tenderly loved by God, may confidently hope for his salvation; for, when such a soul obtains deliverance through his prayers and good works, it incessantly prays for his salvation, and God will deny nothing to such a soul" — St. Alphonsus Liguori.

Reflection: Is there any doubt as to the value of prayers offered for us? Good works, too. Secretly perform some small act of kindness today to benefit a suffering soul.

Eternal rest grant unto them, O Lord, and let perpetual light shine upon them. May they rest in peace. Amen.

Pass It On

I am coming soon; hold fast what you have, so that no
one may seize your crown. — *Revelation 3:11*

"Most of all, the holy souls in purgatory will obtain that the virtues of faith, hope, and love will increase. Faith will open the doors of paradise, and will kindle in us the light of joy that radiates heaven. Hope will lift us away from the mire of the earth and will lead us by the hand to ascend up high. Love, inflaming us with holy ardor will say: 'Come, come!' and in saying so it will give us strength or will carry us in its bosom until we are in the presence of God Most High" — St. Louis Guanella, founder of the Pious Union of St. Joseph in 1924.

Reflection: Pray an Act of Hope: "O my God, relying on your almighty power and infinite mercy and promises, I hope to obtain pardon of my sins, the help of your grace and life everlasting through the merits of Jesus Christ, my Lord and Redeemer. Amen."

Eternal rest grant unto them, O Lord, and let perpetual
light shine upon them. May they rest in peace. Amen.

Suffer Gratefully

"For thou are God of the lowly, helper of the oppressed,
upholder of the weak, protector of the forlorn, savior
of those without hope." — Judith 9:11

"One of the many purposes of suffering in this life is to atone for the temporary, earthly effects of our sins. So instead of kicking and screaming when life's inevitable suffering and sacrifices come your way, embrace them and offer them to expiate your sins (or those of loved ones). Offer even small frustrations to God for atonement, like getting cut off in traffic, or dealing with a grouchy toddler.... One easy way to do this is to make a Morning Offering. Then God can use everything that happens for your spiritual benefit" — Misty Mealey, convert from atheism, author.

Reflection: Begin or renew the habit of saying the Morning Offering daily. You can find it on page 392.

Eternal rest grant unto them, O Lord, and let perpetual
light shine upon them. May they rest in peace. Amen.

Awe and Wonder

*What is man that thou are mindful of him, and the son
of man that thou dost care for him? — Psalm 8:4*

"To the souls in purgatory the Father is protection, security, the infinite tenderness that enfolds. He is that loving Providence who, without [their] realizing, saved them from so many dangers and directed their steps in the way of peace during their days on earth. He has gathered up all life's hours, even those darkened by infidelity of sin — and by his infinite power is now weaving them (through the gradual painful maturation of these souls) into a pattern of such beauty that makes them wonder unceasingly" — Father Hubert, O.F.M. Cap., author.

Reflection: The beauty of heaven is beyond our comprehension. Take one short moment today to give thanks for the beauty of the Lord's creation here and now.

---

*Eternal rest grant unto them, O Lord, and let perpetual
light shine upon them. May they rest in peace. Amen.*

FALL

"It is the welcome apprenticeship to the thoughts, the outlook, the homeliness and joys of Heaven. It is the necessary rehearsal of the eternal orchestra, in which every voice or instrument must be attuned, so that all vibrate in one perfect symphony. It is the abode of hope, and the invention of infinite mercy" — Marie Renè-Bazin, professor, French novelist.

Holy Angels, guardians of those blazing chasms, help me to call to mind those souls, so holy and resigned, from the bowels of the flames that torment them. Make us recognize among them our fathers, our mothers, our sisters, and brothers. Let their cries, so tender and heart-rending, capable of splitting the mountains and mollifying cruelty itself, reach and penetrate our ears.

— Father Charles Arminjon

SEPTEMBER 1

Joyful Penance

"The Lord has need of them." — Matthew 21:3

"In a way, purgatory resembles the state in which St. Francis of Assisi, St. Margaret of Cortona, and St. Augustine found themselves after their conversions. Their thirst for penance was so great that it had to be checked. This spontaneous spirit of penance to make satisfaction to God, this desire to purify oneself, makes one love tribulation and take joy in it, not only in this poor world, but also in the realm of expiation that is purgatory" — Blessed James Alberione, Italian priest, founder of the Daughters of St. Paul and the Society of St. Paul, author.

Reflection: Pray to these saints to give you the grace sufficient to keep the Commandments.

Eternal rest grant unto them, O Lord, and let perpetual light shine upon them. May they rest in peace. Amen.

God's Mercy and Compassion

*Who is a God like thee, pardoning iniquity and passing over
transgression for the remnant of his inheritance? He does not retain his
anger for ever because he delights in steadfast love.* — Micah 7:18

"Eternal Father, turn Your merciful gaze upon the souls suffering in Purgatory, who are enfolded in the Most Compassionate Heart of Jesus. I beg You, by the sorrowful Passion of Jesus Your Son, and by all the bitterness with which His most sacred Soul was flooded, manifest Your mercy to the souls who are under Your just scrutiny. Look upon them in no other way than through the Wounds of Jesus, Your dearly beloved Son; for we firmly believe that there is no limit to Your goodness and compassion. Amen" — St. Faustina (*Diary*, 1227).

Reflection: Do you place limits on God's infinite mercy?

---

*Eternal rest grant unto them, O Lord, and let perpetual
light shine upon them. May they rest in peace. Amen.*

Forgotten Souls

"Put me in remembrance." — *Isaiah 43:26*

"Many persons think so highly of persons consecrated to God that they dispense themselves from the duty of praying for them after they have passed! What a grave error! 'He was so good! Now from heaven he is praying for me,' they say. To think highly of our deceased is charity, but to pray for them is a charity greater, wiser, surer" — St. Augustine.

Reflection: We tend to canonize our departed and envision them already in heaven. Let us refrain from this and instead pray for their souls — a much more prudent choice.

Eternal rest grant unto them, O Lord, and let perpetual light shine upon them. May they rest in peace. Amen.

Pure as Gold

*"He will sit as a refiner and purifier of silver, and he will
purify the sons of Levi and refine them like gold and silver, till
they present right offerings to the Lord." — Malachi 3:3*

"Gold which has been purified to a certain point ceases to suffer any dimi-
nution from the action of fire, however, the fire does not destroy gold, but
only the dross that it may chance to have. In like manner, the divine fire
acts on souls: God holds them in the furnace until every defect has been
burnt away and He has brought them each in His own degree to a certain
standard of perfection. Thus purified, they rest in God without any alloy
of self, they become impassible because there is nothing left to be consumed" — St. Catherine of Genoa.

Reflection: Ask God to purge selfishness from your heart so with
your more open and serving attitude He will find nothing to be
purified.

---

*Eternal rest grant unto them, O Lord, and let perpetual
light shine upon them. May they rest in peace. Amen.*

Resting in Christ's Wounds

*But one of the soldiers pierced his side with a spear, and at
once there came out blood and water. — John 19:34*

"Blessed Teresa of Calcutta once said, 'I'm a little pencil in the hand of a
writing God, who is sending a love letter to the world.' The souls in purgatory send love letters to God, too, interceding for the faithful who are
praying for them. It seems the holy souls are some of God's best friends,
and so, if it is true that we become Christ's friends by imitating Him, then
these wise souls have learned that to be like Christ, they must imitate His
sufferings. This is why the poor souls nestle inside the wound that pierced
Christ's Heart. They rest in the wounds of Christ, their rock and fortress
(Ps 18:2), like the dove which hid itself in the 'clefts of the rock' (Can.
2:14). The holy souls feel the beat of the Sacred Heart and their every
prayer is in perfect sync with the heart rhythm of His love, a love thirsting
for souls" — Father Scott Haynes, S.J.C., author.

Reflection: Contemplate the beating of the Sacred Heart. With each
beat, pray "Jesus, I love You."

---

*Eternal rest grant unto them, O Lord, and let perpetual
light shine upon them. May they rest in peace. Amen.*

Transformation of the Soul

*"Behold the LORD will come in fire ... by fire will the
LORD execute judgment." — Isaiah 66:15-16*

"God sees the soul being purified through the fire of His love returning to
the purity in which He created it, sends forth rays of love which set it on
fire, and draws it to Himself with irresistible force. The soul is so melted
and transformed into God that it seems, as it were, to be only one with
Him. This God of love continues to draw the soul to Himself, to set it on
fire until He has restored it to its original purity" — Father Henri Faure,
S.M., French author.

Reflection: Blessed are the pure of heart, for they shall see God.

---

*Eternal rest grant unto them, O Lord, and let perpetual
light shine upon them. May they rest in peace. Amen.*

A Saturday Devotion

*Continue steadfastly in prayer, being watchful
in it with thanksgiving.* — Colossians 4:2

Venerable Sister Paula of St. Teresa of the Dominican Order had a great devotion to the holy souls in purgatory. Every Saturday she prayed most fervently to the Blessed Virgin. While praying she was rapt in ecstasy and carried to purgatory.

Reflection: One of the many roles of being a parent, grandparent, or godparent is teaching the youngest generation about the holy souls. Bring them to the cemetery on a Saturday. Pray the Eternal Rest Prayer (see below) and have them sprinkle holy water on the graves.

---

*Eternal rest grant unto them, O Lord, and let perpetual
light shine upon them. May they rest in peace. Amen.*

Message of Hope

"As one whom his mother comforts, so I will comfort you." — Isaiah 66:13

"I am the Queen of Heaven," Our Lady said one day to St. Bridget. "I am the Mother of mercy, the sinner's ladder to heaven. There is no pain in purgatory that cannot be made lighter or more endurable by my help. Those who are in purgatory rejoice when they hear my name, like a dying man when he hears some word of hope."

Reflection: Give praise and thanks to God for the earnest intercession of the Blessed Mother. Pray the prayer of St. Germanus: "May the last movement of my tongue be to pronounce the name of the Mother of God. O sweet, O safe is that death which is accompanied and protected by so saying a name; for God only grants the grace of invoking it to those whom He is about to save."

Eternal rest grant unto them, O Lord, and let perpetual light shine upon them. May they rest in peace. Amen.

The Holiness of Brentano

Be filled with the Spirit, addressing one another in psalms
and hymns and spiritual songs and making melody to the
Lord with all your heart. — Ephesians 5:18-19

"A holy Bishop named Brentano was accustomed to recite every day the seven penitential psalms for the souls in purgatory. On one occasion he was kneeling beside a grave in a cemetery reciting them as usual, and at the end of each psalm, as he repeated the Eternal Rest, he heard voices from under the earth answer, *Amen*" — Raphael Bagata, sixteenth-century writer of Church history.

Reflection: Recite the seven penitential psalms from the Bible. They are Psalms 6, 32, 38, 51, 102, 130, and 143. These are the psalms used by the Church to express repentance for sins.

Eternal rest grant unto them, O Lord, and let perpetual
light shine upon them. May they rest in peace. Amen.

Circulation of Love

*"This is my commandment, that you love one
another as I have loved you." — John 15:12*

"In the communion of saints, 'a perennial link of charity exists between the faithful who have already reached their heavenly home, those who are expiating their sins in purgatory and those who are still pilgrims on earth. Between them there is, too, an abundant exchange of all good things.' In this wonderful exchange, the holiness of one profits others, well beyond the harm that the sin of one could cause others. Thus recourse to the communion of saints lets the contrite sinner be more promptly and efficaciously purified of the punishment for sin" — *Catechism of the Catholic Church* (n. 1475).

Reflection: The angels carry to heaven and lay at the foot of the throne of God our prayers and good works, which descend like refreshing dew on the souls in purgatory; and they bring down to us gifts and graces obtained for us by the intercession of the saints. Perform an act charity for an unrepentant sinner.

---

*Eternal rest grant unto them, O Lord, and let perpetual
light shine upon them. May they rest in peace. Amen.*

Catechism of the Little Flower

*Trust in the Lord with all your heart, and do not
rely on your own insight. — Proverbs 3:5*

St. Thérèse of Lisieux, a Doctor of the Church, made an act of oblation
to the merciful love of the good God: "What does this mean for you?
Humility. Complete trust in the merciful love of Jesus. A constant willingness to love Jesus at all times and love of neighbor. The fruits of this
oblation are infinite: A continual purification of the soul, a higher perfection stamped on all the details of life, a constant and ever-more enlight-
ening effusion of truth, and quick entrance into Heaven without passing
through purgatory."

Reflection: Pray with St. Thérèse: "O my God! Most Holy Trinity,
I desire to *Love* You and make You *Loved*, to work for the glory of
Holy Church by saving souls on earth and liberating those suffering souls in purgatory. I desire to accomplish Your will perfectly
and to reach the degree of glory You have prepared for me in Your
Kingdom. I desire, in a word, to be a saint, but I feel my helpless-
ness and I beg You, O my God! to be Yourself my *Sanctity!*" Discover her "Little Way" and offer your prayers and sufferings for the
blessed souls.

---

*Eternal rest grant unto them, O Lord, and let perpetual
light shine upon them. May they rest in peace. Amen.*

Call on Mary

And the virgin's name was Mary. — Luke 1:27

"How good she is to them! A poor sick person, who endures the most acute suffering, is less comforted by words of consolation than are the souls in purgatory by the very name of *Mary*. This name of hope and salvation which they love to invoke brings down upon them the pitying gaze of their loving mother; and as she offers to God her prayers for their relief, there descends upon those poor souls a dew of heavenly consolation" — St. Vincent Ferrer.

Reflection: Repeat "Mary" devoutly several times, confident that she will intercede for our departed loved ones. Pray: "O Mary, Mother of God, flood all of humanity with the graces of your burning love, now and at the hour of our death." In every danger of forfeiting divine grace, we should think of Mary, and invoke her name, together with that of Jesus; for these two names always go together. Many saints died repeating Jesus and Mary on their lips. Let us beg God to grant that at our death the names of Jesus and Mary may be the last words on our lips.

Eternal rest grant unto them, O Lord, and let perpetual light shine upon them. May they rest in peace. Amen.

Not a Prison

By his wounds you have been healed. — *1 Peter 2:24*

"As I studied to be a Catholic, the official teaching about purgatory made sense to me.... I have only grown in my appreciation of purgatory over time as a Catholic. It is unfortunate that Catholic imagination has sometimes negatively embellished upon the reality of purgatory which is actually revealed as a very positive and benign process of healing and forgiveness.... I see purgatory as really a kind of 'divine therapy' where God's love heals us entirely for the life and love of heaven" — Father John, Anglican convert.

Reflection: Ask the Lord to bring healing and wholeness to your ancestors.

Eternal rest grant unto them, O Lord, and let perpetual light shine upon them. May they rest in peace. Amen.

Stargazing

The moon and the stars rule over the night, for his
steadfast love endures for ever. — Psalm 136:9

"Perhaps these souls are like stars in the night. Perhaps each is dark in its own eyes but who knows if it does not shed light upon the others? It is here that justice and peace have kissed each other. To all that justice wills, or says or does, in purgatory peace answers, and peace alone. These souls offer to God, who purifies them, the same Amen which the souls of the blessed in heaven offer to God who glorifies them. Their whole existence echoes the everlasting song of heaven — 'Holy, holy, holy, Lord God of Hosts. Heaven and earth are full of your glory. Hosanna in the Highest'" — Monsignor Gay, French priest.

Reflection: When you gaze upon the stars at night, remember the countless souls in need of prayer.

Eternal rest grant unto them, O Lord, and let perpetual
light shine upon them. May they rest in peace. Amen.

Do Not Despair

Thou preparest a table before me in the presence of my enemies;
Thou anointest my head with oil, my cup overflows ... and I shall
dwell in the house of the LORD forever. — Psalm 23:5-6

"Peter was being tormented by the possibility that his younger sister committed suicide. If it was true, Peter knew that she would never attain heaven, for she had committed the unforgivable sin — despair. But was this prohibition accurate?

"I had almost forgotten about Peter when he and a group of young adults showed up one evening. Peter was a changed man, and a little questioning revealed why. He had been having frequent dreams about his sister, he told us. In each, instead of her shabby gray wardrobe she wore lovely gowns, and a table behind her was set with banquet linens and fine china.

"Peter's sister seemed to understand. 'Those of us here lost our opportunities to make the world a better place,' she explained. 'But there is no despair, and although we will need more time, we will eventually reach eternity. In the meantime, the banquet serves as a reminder of what lies ahead'" — Joan Wester Anderson, author.

Reflection: Pray for a suffering soul who gave into despair.

Eternal rest grant unto them, O Lord, and let perpetual
light shine upon them. May they rest in peace. Amen.

Fervor and Zeal

"Come with me and see my zeal for the LORD." — *2 Kings 10:16*

St. Gertrude asked Our Lord: "How many souls, O Lord, does your mercy condescend to deliver in answer to the prayers of each of us?" His response was: "I deliver more or less, according to the zeal of each nun and the fervor of her prayers."

Reflection: Pray with fervor and zeal for the chosen servants of God. They depend on it.

Eternal rest grant unto them, O Lord, and let perpetual light shine upon them. May they rest in peace. Amen.

Bowls of Charity

"Your reward shall be very great." — Genesis 15:1

"Whatever we offer in charity for the dead is changed into merit for ourselves, and we will receive a hundredfold after death. We should not be afraid of exercising Christian charity towards the souls in purgatory. When we work for them, we work for ourselves. We lay up treasure of which God will give us the benefit in our day of tribulation. We are ensuring a favorable reception for our own soul when our last hour comes. It may be that by the intercession of the souls that we have helped God will give us such perfect contrition as will suffice for the entire remission of the temporal punishment due to our sins, and that He will enable us to gain a plenary indulgence at the hour of death" — St. Ambrose.

Reflection: Pray from your heart. Offer an act of contrition to God, seeking forgiveness (see page 390).

Eternal rest grant unto them, O Lord, and let perpetual light shine upon them. May they rest in peace. Amen.

The Doorkeeper's Deliverance

Out of the depths I cry to thee, O Lord!
Lord, hear my voice! — Psalm 130:1

St. John Macias' charity and zeal for the souls in purgatory were so pleasing to God that He permitted multitudes of souls to appear to John. Once a vast throng of souls, like doves soaring heavenward, came to him expressing thanks for their liberation, while a host of others appeared in agony. He would hear pitiful cries: "Friar John, how long must we remain in so much suffering? Pray for me ... for me ... for me! I have greater need! Commend us to God!" He redoubled his prayers and sprinkled more holy water.

Reflection: Pitiful sighs. Moans and trembling in purgatory. Have profound compassion for the agonizing souls. Be their deliverers. Pray constantly: "Jesus, Son of David, have mercy on the holy souls."

Eternal rest grant unto them, O Lord, and let perpetual
light shine upon them. May they rest in peace. Amen.

Holy Vow for Holy Heroes

"And then he will send out the angels, and gather his elect from the four winds, from the ends of the earth to the ends of heaven." — Mark 13:27

"The nuns of the Convent of St. Catherine, at Naples, had a pious habit of reciting every evening the Office of the Dead for the relief of the departed. This practice was as precious to purgatory as it was blessed by heaven. One day an extraordinary occurrence had prolonged the work of the community until late at night, and the nuns went to sleep without having said the Office. While they slept, angels descended from heaven, and took their places in the choir, singing the Office of the Dead with heavenly harmonies. The Venerable Sister Paula of St. Teresa was awake, and at prayer in her cell. Surprised by the unusual music, and thinking that the community must be assembled in the choir, she hastened to the church. What was her surprise to see angels equal in number to the number of nuns supplementing their work of charity, so that the departed should not be for one day deprived of the benefit of the Office! Moved to tears by this manifestation of sympathy by the angels for the souls in purgatory, the venerable servant of God vowed to be particularly fervent from that day forward in prayer for the faithful departed" — *Life of Venerable Paula of St. Teresa.*

Reflection: In spiritual solidarity, unite your prayers with the angels and saints to make those prayers even more powerful.

Eternal rest grant unto them, O Lord, and let perpetual light shine upon them. May they rest in peace. Amen.

Admonition from the Lord

*Faith is the assurance of things hoped for, the
conviction of things not seen.* — Hebrews 11:1

One day St. Gertrude was praying for the holy souls when Jesus admonished her for not praying with confident assurance, the faith and realized hope that God hears and answers our prayers. He assured her: "It would not be past My Justice to release those suffering souls for whom you are praying, immediately, if you would pray with confidence for this petition."

Reflection: Give someone the St. Gertrude Prayer on a prayer card. Pray: "Eternal Father, I offer Thee the Most Precious Blood of Thy Divine Son, Jesus, in union with the Masses said throughout the world today, for all the holy souls in purgatory, for sinners everywhere, for sinners in the Universal Church, those in my own home and within my family. Amen."

---

*Eternal rest grant unto them, O Lord, and let perpetual
light shine upon them. May they rest in peace. Amen.*

Eight Beatitudes of Indulgences

Have mercy on me, O God, according to thy steadfast love; according to thy abundant mercy blot out my transgressions. — *Psalm 51:1*

"They keep us among the thoughts of the purgative way.
"They keep an unworldly effect on us.
"They keep the doctrine of purgatory before us.
"They are an exercise of charity to the faithful departed.
"They are a means of promoting God's glory.
"They honor the satisfaction of Jesus, Mary and the Saints.
"They deepen our views of sin and give us a great horror of it.
"They keep us in harmony with the spirit of the church"
— Father Frederick Faber, convert, English hymn writer, theologian, author.

Reflection: The word "indulgence" comes from the Latin *indulgentia*, which means to be kind or tender. God lavishes His tender mercy on us with the treasury of indulgences. Be greedy for God's grace today. Indulge in indulgences!

Eternal rest grant unto them, O Lord, and let perpetual light shine upon them. May they rest in peace. Amen.

Our Purgatory Mission

*Have no anxiety about anything, but in everything by
prayer and supplication with thanksgiving let your requests
be made known to God. — Philippians 4:6*

"The holy souls are eager for the prayers of the faithful, which can gain indulgences for them. Their intercession is powerful. It is unbelievable what they can do for our spiritual good, out of gratitude they have towards those on earth who remember to pray for them. Pray unceasingly. We must empty purgatory!" — St. Pio of Pietrelcina.

Reflection: Pray for those who did the most for the release of the deceased souls.

---

*Eternal rest grant unto them, O Lord, and let perpetual
light shine upon them. May they rest in peace. Amen.*

Avoid Pileups

Whatever a man sows, that he will also reap. — *Galatians 6:7*

"Some people live in such a distracted fashion that, when they take some time out in the evening to look over the day, they discover a great many of these defects sprinkled through it (inconsiderate words, excessive curiosity, bursts of anger, acts of pride, of stinginess, of gluttony) and so the list goes on. Unfortunately they are often dismissed as trifles or confessed without real sorrow, and so these people are piling up debts with the justice of God" — St. Louis Guanella, founder of the Pious Union of St. Joseph in 1924.

Reflection: Shave off these vices from your life.

Eternal rest grant unto them, O Lord, and let perpetual light shine upon them. May they rest in peace. Amen.

Power to Pardon

The king again said to Esther, "What is your petition,
Queen Esther? It shall be granted you." — Esther 7:2

"I am like a prince full of affection for some of his subjects who have been thrown into prison by his authority and for good reason, and yet unwilling to use his sovereign power to pardon them, and thus interfere with the ordinary course of justice; but quite ready to show mercy if some noble of his Court would intercede, and make satisfaction for the offenders. I willingly accept all that is offered me on behalf of the souls in purgatory, and make it an occasion to release them from their sufferings, and put them in possession of everlasting happiness" — Our Lord to St. Gertrude.

Reflection: Surrender to God total control of everything today.

Eternal rest grant unto them, O Lord, and let perpetual
light shine upon them. May they rest in peace. Amen.

Creating Heavenly Friends

Brethren, pray for us. — 1 Thessalonians 5:25

Besides deep faith in God, Venerable Solanus Casey showed a great devotion to the Communion of Saints, which centered in Mary. It also included those who had preceded him (deceased loved ones). Consequently, he had a great devotion to the poor souls. Father Solanus told people: "If we, by our prayers and sacrifices, freed a soul from purgatory, we would then have another intercessor for us in heaven."

Reflection: Remember, when you pray for the holy souls you gain fresh intercessors and increase their intercessory power. Make friends in high places — deliver the holy souls!

Eternal rest grant unto them, O Lord, and let perpetual light shine upon them. May they rest in peace. Amen.

The Presence of Souls

*[T]he soul of Jonathan was knit to the soul of David, and
Jonathan loved him as his own soul. — 1 Samuel 18:1*

"Every time I pray for my departed friends, I seem to feel them near me,
and the thought gives me the same pleasure as their presence during life;
it is as if there were only a veil between us, and the least effort would be
enough to tear it down" — Blessed Frédéric Ozanam.

Reflection: Light candles for your departed friends. St. Charles Bor-
romeo tells us: "The candle that gives light to others must itself be
consumed. Thus we also have to act. We ourselves are consumed to
give good example to others."

*Eternal rest grant unto them, O Lord, and let perpetual
light shine upon them. May they rest in peace. Amen.*

What Is Purgatory?

So shun youthful passions and aim at righteousness,
faith, love and peace, along with those who call upon
the Lord from a pure heart. — *2 Timothy 2:22*

"Purgatory, often imagined as a place, is actually a condition. Someone who dies in God's grace (and therefore at peace with God and men) but who still needs purification before he can see God face to face is in purgatory.

"When Peter had betrayed Jesus, the Lord turned around and looked at Peter: 'And Peter went out and wept bitterly' — a feeling like being in purgatory. Just such a purgatory probably awaits most of us at the moment of our death: the Lord looks at us full of love and we experience burning shame and painful remorse over our wicked or 'merely' unloving behavior. Only after this purifying pain will we be capable of meeting his loving gaze in untroubled heavenly joy" — *YOUCAT* (*Youth Catechism of the Catholic Church*, nn. 158-159).

Reflection: Resolve to always flee sin rather than give in to temptation. The holy souls are ready to assist!

Eternal rest grant unto them, O Lord, and let perpetual
light shine upon them. May they rest in peace. Amen.

Thirst Is Quenched

*Whoever drinks of the water that I shall give
him will never thirst. — John 4:14*

A document called the *Passion of Perpetua and Felicity*, martyrs of the early Church, described St. Perpetua's vision regarding her deceased seven-year-old brother, Dinocrates, who died of tissue cancer. She saw him in a gloomy place, pale in color. He was parched and thirsty.

Dinocrates was trying to reach a pool of water, but it was too high for him because of his stature. St. Perpetua prayed with groans and weeping for him. In another vision, he was happy drinking from the pool incessantly and was satisfied. The vision is symbolic, representing the water of eternal life that quenches the thirst of the soul.

Reflection: When you sign yourself using holy water next time you enter church, renew your baptismal vows and your commitment to renounce sin, selfishness, and the devil's pomps and lies and to strive to become a saint.

---

*Eternal rest grant unto them, O Lord, and let perpetual
light shine upon them. May they rest in peace. Amen.*

Perfect Servants of God

For he will give his angels charge of you to
guard you in all your ways. — Psalm 91:11

"The Guardian Angels conduct the souls into purgatory. They encourage us to pray for the suffering souls, and inform the holy souls what persons are fulfilling this charitable office. The life of Venerable Agnes of Jesus lived in constant communication with the holy angels. We see these faithful friends making intercession for their clients, and bringing to them in the midst of their suffering refreshment for which they groan, leading them to heaven in a magnificent procession when their time of expiation is complete" — Father Henri Faure, S.M., French author.

Reflection: Offer this prayer to the guardian angels for yourself and your deceased loved ones: "St. Michael, St. Raphael, St. Gabriel, protect us. Assist us with your angels. Help us and pray for us. Amen."

Eternal rest grant unto them, O Lord, and let perpetual
light shine upon them. May they rest in peace. Amen.

Remember That You Will Die

"Repent, for the kingdom of heaven is at hand." — *Matthew 3:2*

"O you, whose lives are so lax, who do not fear to stain yourselves with a thousand faults in order to please the world or spare your body a moment's trouble, tell us:

"Have you understood the mystery of God's justice, and have you meditated upon the length of the torments that await you?" — Father Charles Arminjon, French preacher, author.

Reflection: Contemplate God's justice.

Eternal rest grant unto them, O Lord, and let perpetual light shine upon them. May they rest in peace. Amen.

OCTOBER 1

Life's Main Purpose

"For with God nothing will be impossible." — *Luke 1:37*

The Little Flower, St. Thérèse of Lisieux, said that when she died there would be nothing left for her to burn (purify) in purgatory. Her life of love and sacrifice for the Lord would be the holocaust that would make purgatory unnecessary.

Reflection: Let us work now while we can with our prayers and sacrifices in order to avoid purgatory later.

Eternal rest grant unto them, O Lord, and let perpetual light shine upon them. May they rest in peace. Amen.

Messengers of Good Tidings and Peace

Are they not all ministering spirits sent forth to serve, for the
sake of those who are to obtain salvation? — Hebrews 1:14

"The holy angels constantly minister to the souls in purgatory to give them intelligence of the prayers and satisfaction which are offered for those in the Church on earth, and thus to let them know that they are not forgotten, and that the time of their detention is to be shortened. In this respect they are in truth messengers of good tidings and of peace, which they so much delight to be. Moreover, it is probable that the holy angels are the sources from whom proceed a thousand suggestions to us to pray for the holy souls, sudden remembrances of them, feelings as if they were near and in need of our prayers" — Father H. J. Coleridge, S.J., preacher, author.

Reflection: Pray: "Holy Angel, my light, enlighten me." Attend Mass in honor of your guardian angel.

Eternal rest grant unto them, O Lord, and let perpetual
light shine upon them. May they rest in peace. Amen.

OCTOBER 3

Don't Bet on Purgatory

"Enter by the narrow gate; for the gate is wide and the way is easy, that leads to destruction, and those who enter by it are many. For the gate is narrow and the way is hard, that leads to life, and those who find it are few." — Matthew 7:13-14

"Sometimes what holds us back from responding wholeheartedly in our present circumstances is believing that we don't have to focus too much on that right now, because it will be taken care of in purgatory. But if we aim for purgatory and miss, there really isn't a good backup available" — Ralph Martin, president of Renewal Ministries, professor, author.

Reflection: Mercy on the exiled souls will bring us also the crowning mercy of a holy death.

Eternal rest grant unto them, O Lord, and let perpetual light shine upon them. May they rest in peace. Amen.

Partner with St. Francis

*For those whom he foreknew he also predestined to be
conformed to the image of his Son, in order that he might be
the first-born among many brethren.* — *Romans 8:29*

"Our Lord said to St. Francis: I grant to you that every year, on the anniversary of your death, you shall go to purgatory, and all the souls you shall find there of your three orders ... and of the others who shall have remained sincerely devoted to you, you shall deliver by virtue of your Stigmas, and will lead them into the glories of Paradise so they may be conformed to me in your death, as you have been in your life" — Raphael Brown, Franciscan tertiary, author.

Reflection: Pray the prayer attributed to St. Francis. "Lord, make me an instrument of your peace; where there is hatred let me sow love; where there is injury, pardon; where there is doubt, faith; where there is despair, hope; where there is darkness, light; and where there is sadness, joy. O Divine Master, grant that I may not so much seek to be consoled, as to console; to be understood, as to understand; to be loved, as to love; for it is in giving that we receive, it is in pardoning that we are pardoned, and it is in dying that we are born to eternal life."

---

*Eternal rest grant unto them, O Lord, and let perpetual
light shine upon them. May they rest in peace. Amen.*

OCTOBER 5

Mortification of Curiosity

When Peter saw him, he said to Jesus, "Lord what about this man?" Jesus said to him, "If it is my will that he remain until I come, what is that to you? Follow me!" — John 21:21-22

"On the evening of that same day, when I had already gone to bed, a certain soul came to me, woke me up by tapping on the night table and asked me to pray for her. I wanted to ask who she was, but I mortified my curiosity and joined this little mortification to my prayer and offered them for her" — St. Faustina (*Diary*, 516).

Reflection: Fast from idle curiosity and whenever you awaken during the night, offer a short prayer for the blessed souls.

Eternal rest grant unto them, O Lord, and let perpetual light shine upon them. May they rest in peace. Amen.

Silent Voices

"Give heed to him and hearken to his voice, do not rebel
against him, for he will not pardon your transgression;
for my name is in him." — Exodus 23:21

"I fell asleep praying the Office of Readings, which priests and religious are required to follow every day. Then, I heard somebody say my name, and I immediately woke up.... Whether it's a guardian angel or a soul in purgatory, I don't know. I just know somebody is keeping track of me. I think these experiences are in harmony with the Church's understanding of the Communion of Saints, which is the spiritual family we belong to as the Church Militant, the Church Suffering and the Church Triumphant. This is the abiding spiritual kinship that we share with all souls in a state of grace, which transcends earthly ties.

"The way I look at it, then, there are souls who take an interest in me, and they may be trying to get my attention when I pray. I often wonder, but I sometimes think the voices I hear are my ancestors and deceased friends who pray for me as I pray for them. We can think of it as part of the marvelous spiritual exchange made possible because of the Communion of Saints. And it's our commitment to pray that fosters this spiritual bond" — Father Dan Cambra, M.I.C., director, Holy Souls Sodality.

Reflection: Pray Psalm 130, *"De Profundis,"* the Church's official Prayer for Dead (see page 393), in honor of the souls in purgatory.

Eternal rest grant unto them, O Lord, and let perpetual
light shine upon them. May they rest in peace. Amen.

Ladder to Heaven

My brethren, if anyone among you wanders from the truth and some one brings him back, let him know that whoever brings back a sinner from the error of his way will save his soul from death and will cover a multitude of sins. — James 5:19

"Blessed Alanus writes that many of the brethren had appeared to them while reciting the rosary, and had declared that next to the Holy Sacrifice of the Mass there was no more powerful means than the Rosary to help the suffering souls. Numerous souls were released daily who otherwise would have been obliged to remain in purgatory for years" — St. Alphonsus Liguori.

Reflection: The Rosary is linked to our own lives and destiny. Our Lady of Fátima told the seers to pray the rosary for peace and the conversion of sinners. The reason the Rosary is so powerful to obtain relief for the holy souls is because of the indulgences attached to these prayers. Can you refuse this heartfelt devotion? Pray the Rosary from the heart.

Eternal rest grant unto them, O Lord, and let perpetual light shine upon them. May they rest in peace. Amen.

Purgatory's Three Essential Joys

*Night shall be no more; they need no light of lamp or
sun, for the Lord God will be their light, and they shall
reign for ever and ever. — Revelation 22:5*

"The three essential joys of purgatory are these:

"First, the certainty of their salvation. The holy souls know they are confirmed in grace, unable to sin or to be lost.

"The second joy of purgatory consists in expiation of one's faults. Sin constitutes a loathsome filth in the soul, a sort of spiritual leprosy. If the cleansing of festering wounds brings relief, how much more must the soul in purgatory feel, who, having passed into eternity, now knows the ugliness of sin. Sin is insult, offense, injury to the majesty and holiness of God.

"The third joy is love of God. Love makes every sacrifice easier. The souls in purgatory love God with the most intense affection — and love desires sacrifice and immolation" — Blessed James Alberione, Italian priest, founder of the Daughters of St. Paul and the Society of St. Paul, author.

Reflection: Sin is a stain that prevents us from entering into the presence of God. Examine your life to address any faults that come between you and the Lord.

---

*Eternal rest grant unto them, O Lord, and let perpetual
light shine upon them. May they rest in peace. Amen.*

Seek the Last Place

"So the last will be first, and the first last." — Matthew 20:16

"I would rather occupy one of the last places in that sojourn of security than possess all the uncertain and deceiving joys of this world!" — Father Frederick Faber, convert, English hymn writer, theologian, author.

Reflection: Earthly pleasures can be fleeting and sometimes give us a false sense of what is important in life. Pray that when challenges present themselves you will offer them up for the benefit of the holy souls.

Eternal rest grant unto them, O Lord, and let perpetual light shine upon them. May they rest in peace. Amen.

OCTOBER 10

Voluntary "Satispassion"

This is evidence of the righteous judgment of God, that
you may be made worthy of the kingdom of God, for
which you are suffering. — 2 *Thessalonians* 1:5

"Voluntary acceptance of the pains of purgatory obtains for the poor souls the remission of their debt to divine justice. But, whereas on earth the satisfaction is meritorious, the 'satispassion' [a term used by theologians, meaning patiently suffering the demands of God's justice] in purgatory is no longer meritorious. Purgatory is a place of *satispassion*, which applies what was lacking on the earth in line of satisfaction (doing penance, works of mercy)" — Mother Mary of St. Austin, Helpers of the Holy Souls, author.

Reflection: What can we do now, voluntarily, to assist those in purgatory? Instead of trying to avoid pains and sufferings, offer them up for the holy souls.

Eternal rest grant unto them, O Lord, and let perpetual
light shine upon them. May they rest in peace. Amen.

Suffering for Divine Love

I have been crucified with Christ. — Galatians 2:20

"The poor souls are spiritually crucified. They may say: 'I am crucified in this flame.' But the sense of the word is contrary to the sense it has for the damned. Here it means the living flame of love, which ceases not to mount up to God" — St. John of the Cross.

Reflection: Light a candle for the souls today, and as the flame reaches heavenward, contemplate the awesome love of God.

Eternal rest grant unto them, O Lord, and let perpetual light shine upon them. May they rest in peace. Amen.

Reward for the Wholehearted

*But I do not account my life of any value nor as precious to myself, if only
I may accomplish my course and the ministry which I received from the
Lord Jesus, to testify to the gospel of the grace of God.* — Acts 20:24

"Purgatory is for those who were not wholehearted enough in doing what
their hearts told them they should do. They died having accomplished part
of the work God asked of them, but not all. It is his merciful option for
the incomplete, not those who reject him altogether" — Father Michael J.
Taylor, S.J., Scripture scholar, author.

Reflection: Invoke the holy souls to help you discern the deepest
desire of your heart.

---

*Eternal rest grant unto them, O Lord, and let perpetual
light shine upon them. May they rest in peace. Amen.*

OCTOBER 13

Prayers Unlock Prison Doors

*"Give to him who begs from you, and do not refuse him
who would borrow from you."* — *Matthew 5:42*

"The poor souls are in a fiery prison, and our good God, to open that prison, asks only a prayer from us. Can we refuse this prayer?" — Blessed Mary of Providence, foundress of the Helpers of the Holy Souls.

Reflection: The prison of purgatory is one of our own making. The fire is the longing to be in the presence of the Lord. The key to release is prayer. Pray for those suffering souls whose own prayers can no longer help bring them to the Love they so intensely desire.

---

*Eternal rest grant unto them, O Lord, and let perpetual
light shine upon them. May they rest in peace. Amen.*

Walking with the Souls

Angels came and ministered to him. — Matthew 4:11

"Private revelations attest to Guardian Angels' visits to purgatory. St. Margaret Mary's Guardian Angel said to her: 'Come, let us walk in purgatory.' He led her to a place where she saw a great number of poor souls in human form who raised their arms to her and implored mercy. She saw many angels there, consoling them, and she knew that they were the Guardian Angels" — Father Pietro Louvet, French author.

Reflection: Angels bring hope to the weary, always pointing us upward toward heaven, promising us that at the end of this earthly pilgrimage they will be there to carry us to the splendor of our heavenly home. Pray: "Holy angel, my helper, comfort me."

Eternal rest grant unto them, O Lord, and let perpetual light shine upon them. May they rest in peace. Amen.

OCTOBER 15

Souls' Work Leads to Success

"Give, and it will be given to you; good measure, pressed down, shaken together, running over, will be put into your lap. For the measure you give will be the measure you get back." — Luke 6:38

"Work for the suffering souls is sure of success. As they cannot be lost, our work for them must bear fruit. To obtain for these souls the greatest of all gifts, God seen face to face, will, at the same time, increase the accidental joy of our Lord, of His Blessed Mother, and of the saints" — Father Frederick Faber, convert, English hymn writer, theologian, author.

Reflection: Joyfully endure some annoyance or discomfort for the sake of the souls. Remember that the souls find joy in knowing that they are not lost and will someday be in the presence of the Lord.

Eternal rest grant unto them, O Lord, and let perpetual light shine upon them. May they rest in peace. Amen.

Out of Reach

*My soul waits for the LORD more than
watchmen for the morning. — Psalm 130:6*

"We often hear it said that in the souls in purgatory there is an ebb and flow. Strongly drawn toward God, they are held back by the 'remains of sin,' which they have to expiate. They cannot rush to the goal which they so ardently desire. Love of God does not diminish their pain, but increases it. And this love is no longer meritorious. How eloquent is their title: The Suffering Church!"— Father Reginald Garrigou-Lagrange, O.P., French theologian, author.

Reflection: Help members of the Church Suffering fulfill their longing for God. Free your heart from desires, senses, affections, attitudes, or whatever could ensnare your soul in order to free the suffering souls.

---

*Eternal rest grant unto them, O Lord, and let perpetual
light shine upon them. May they rest in peace. Amen.*

Gratitude Lives in Heaven

*The LORD is my shepherd, I shall not want; he makes
me lie down in green pastures. He leads me beside still
waters; he restores my soul. — Psalm 23:1-3*

"On awakening this morning on the Sunday of the Good Shepherd, two of my suffering friends came to take leave of me; today the Good Shepherd received them into His eternal home. They left with untold joy and happiness. When I asked them to remember me, they replied: 'Ingratitude has never entered heaven'" — St. Margaret Mary Alacoque.

Reflection: Have a grateful heart today and always. Using the Rosary recite: "Thank you, Jesus!"

---

*Eternal rest grant unto them, O Lord, and let perpetual
light shine upon them. May they rest in peace. Amen.*

Justice and Peace

"But the tax collector, standing far off, would not even lift up his eyes to heaven, but beat his breast saying, 'God, be merciful to me a sinner!'" — *Luke 18:13*

"Let the penitent always feel pain for his sin, and always feel joy for his pain. In the words of the Psalmist: 'Justice and peace have kissed.' Such is the liturgy of the Church Suffering" — St. Augustine.

Reflection: Blessed Paul VI's apostolic constitution *Indulgentiarum Doctrina* says: "It is a divinely revealed truth that sins bring punishments inflicted by God's sanctity and justice. These must be expiated either on this earth through the sorrows, miseries and calamities of this life and above all through death, or else in the life beyond through fire and torments or 'purifying' punishments.... These punishments are imposed by the just and merciful judgment of God for the purification of souls, the defense of the sanctity of the moral order and the restoration of the glory of God to its full majesty" (n. 2).

Eternal rest grant unto them, O Lord, and let perpetual light shine upon them. May they rest in peace. Amen.

The Way of the Cross in Purgatory

And he is the expiation for our sins, and not for ours only
but also for the sins of the whole world. — 1 John 2:2

"Mary Magdalene ... stood before the Cross like a living mirror, without movement, her eyes lifted to Him. The sublimity of the revelation she received there surpasses all word, all thought, all sentiment.

"Christ's unspeakable holiness, His measureless pain, His radiating peace, wrapped her round. These three hours on Calvary were her purgatory. But she would not have given one moment of this pain for all the joys of Tabor. In Our Lord and through Him she expiated her own faults, while all thought of herself disappeared.

"She was immersed in the contemplation of the Word made flesh, suffering for the sins of the world. In Him rather than herself, she understood what sin means for God and for man. Surely here we have an image of the souls in purgatory.

"Calvary shows how divine light penetrates purgatorial darkness. It shows divine light radiating these silent souls with all the pains of Jesus crucified. Purgatorial pain and peace are found also on the earth, beneath the holiness of Him who takes away the sins of the world" — Mother Mary of St. Austin, Helpers of the Holy Souls, author.

Reflection: For a special favor, pray the Way of the Cross for the holy souls for thirty-three days in honor of the thirty-three years of Our Lord's life.

Eternal rest grant unto them, O Lord, and let perpetual
light shine upon them. May they rest in peace. Amen.

Let Not Love Be Lost

If I speak in the tongues of men and of angels, but have not love,
I am a noisy gong or a clanging cymbal. — 1 Corinthians 13:1

"Purgatory is a place not only where the love of God tempers the justice of God, but where the love of man may temper the injustice of man. Most men and women are quite unconscious of the injustice, the ingratitude, and the thanklessness of their lives until the cold hand of death is laid upon one that they love. It is then, and only then, that they realize (and oh, with what regret!) the haunting poverty of their love and kindness" — Venerable Archbishop Fulton J. Sheen.

Reflection: Offer a special prayer of thanksgiving for loved ones, living and deceased.

Eternal rest grant unto them, O Lord, and let perpetual
light shine upon them. May they rest in peace. Amen.

The Power of the Our Father

"When you pray, say: 'Father, hallowed be thy name. Thy kingdom come. Give us each day our daily bread; and forgive us our sins, for we ourselves forgive every one who is indebted to us; and lead us not into temptation.'" — Luke 11:2-4

"One of the first companions of St. Francis, Brother Corrado, was known for his spirit of prayer. He directed a youth whose prayer life was weak, but with Brother Corrado's direction he became a model of holiness. Soon after his conversion he died. While praying before the altar Brother Corrado heard his voice asking for prayers. 'I died a holy death and am saved but I had not time to expiate. I am suffering a terrible chastisement.' Brother Corrado immediately prayed before the tabernacle an Our Father and Eternal Rest. 'Oh my good Father, how much good your prayer does for me! I entreat you to continue. I experience the most intense relief when you pray.' Brother Corrado, kneeling, repeated the Our Father one hundred times. In unspeakable joy, the soul said: 'I thank you, my dear Father, in the name of God, for I am delivered; behold I am about to enter the Kingdom of Heaven'" — Sister M. Emmanuel, O.S.B., author.

Reflection: When passing a Catholic Church, spiritually send your guardian angel inside to pray at the foot of the altar to plead for the delivery of the suffering souls.

Eternal rest grant unto them, O Lord, and let perpetual light shine upon them. May they rest in peace. Amen.

OCTOBER 22

Everything Is an Eternal Present

*O the depth of the riches and wisdom and knowledge
of God! How unsearchable are his judgments and
how inscrutable his ways! — Romans 11:33*

"You and I both die and through the good fortune and the goodness and mercy of the Lord we are obliged to stay in purgatory for 100 years. During those years nobody thinks of Padre Pio to have Masses offered. For Our Lord, the past does not exist; the future does not exist. Everything is an eternal present. Those prayers have already been taken into account so that even now I can pray for the happy death of my great-grandfather! Do you really think the Lord needs our bureaucracy?" — St. Pio of Pietrelcina.

Reflection: Pray for those throughout the world who have died with no one to pray for them. Remember in a special way government leaders.

---

*Eternal rest grant unto them, O Lord, and let perpetual
light shine upon them. May they rest in peace. Amen.*

The Stumbling Block of Lukewarmness

*"So because you are lukewarm, and neither hot nor cold,
I will spew you out of my mouth." — Revelation 3:16*

"Another cause for purgatory is lukewarmness and it is the most common. Someone who was cold or indifferent in the service of God and had no spiritual warmth or generosity cannot possibly go from this life into the heavenly light, into the union that God desires to have with it. Lukewarmness is shown in the way we examine our conscience, say Rosaries, attend Mass and receive Holy Communion" — Blessed James Alberione, Italian priest, founder of the Daughters of St. Paul and the Society of St. Paul, author.

Reflection: Pray this prayer to overcome lukewarmness: "Since you, O my Jesus, have been so liberal with your graces toward me and have deigned to give your Blood and your life for me, I am sorry for having acted with so little generosity toward you, who are worthy of all honor and all love. But, O my Jesus, you know my weakness; help me with your powerful grace. In you I confide, O Immaculate Virgin Mary, help me to overcome myself and to become a saint. Amen."

*Eternal rest grant unto them, O Lord, and let perpetual
light shine upon them. May they rest in peace. Amen.*

In the Hand of God

But the souls of the righteous are in the hand of God,
and no torment will ever touch them. — Wisdom 3:1

"Whoever follows Jesus in this life is welcome where he has preceded us. Therefore, as we visit the cemeteries, let us remember that resting in those tombs are merely the mortal remains of our dear ones who await the final resurrection. Their souls, as Scripture tells us, are already 'in the hand of God' (Wis 3:1). Thus, the most proper and effective way to honor them is to pray for them, offering acts of faith, hope and charity. In union with the Eucharistic Sacrifice, we can intercede for their eternal salvation and experience the most profound communion in the expectation of being together, enjoying forever the Love which created and redeemed us" — Pope Benedict XVI (Angelus, November 1, 2009).

Reflection: Whenever you see a dedication memorial recite the Eternal Rest Prayer (see below).

Eternal rest grant unto them, O Lord, and let perpetual
light shine upon them. May they rest in peace. Amen.

How to Pass Up Purgatory

*"Not everyone who says to me, 'Lord, Lord,' shall enter
the kingdom of heaven, but he who does the will of my
Father who is in heaven." — Matthew 7:21*

"It is not God's wish that we go to purgatory. We are given the grace to avoid purgatory. How? Doing God's will in all things. Avoiding sin. Forgiving. Doing penance. Frequent Confession and Holy Communion. Asking for the grace to avoid purgatory. Accept sufferings. Deliver the holy souls." — Father Paul O'Sullivan, O.P., author.

Reflection: We need to learn from purgatory so we can empty purgatory and avoid purgatory!

*Eternal rest grant unto them, O Lord, and let perpetual
light shine upon them. May they rest in peace. Amen.*

Sowing Kindness

"Therefore you must also be ready; for the Son of man is coming at an hour you do not expect." — Matthew 24:44

J. R. R. Tolkien's "Leaf by Niggle" is a story about an artist whose main goal is to paint a great tree. He starts by painting a single leaf and then adds more details: more leaves, branches, birds, hills. Soon Niggle is taking time off from his work to paint. When he aids a needy neighbor, a gardener named Parish who is lame and has a sick wife, Niggle takes even more time off from his work and his painting.

During this time Niggle gets sick. Niggle's illness worsens, and he must go to an institution where he can heal. While he is healing he performs humble labor. In due course he is healed and returns to the forest to work as a gardener. Over time Niggle realizes that he is working in the forest of his painting. His painting tried to capture the majesty of this forest, but now he sees how pale his drawing is compared with the magnificence of the actual forest. As time passes, Niggle is reunited with his neighbor Parish. Now they join forces as gardeners working in the most magnificent of forests.

Reflection: We cannot capture the magnificence of heaven, but we can get ready to enter heaven by doing that which is good and that which drives us to be who we are. As we sow kindness, our garden of good deeds grows and we become more prepared to heal and eventually enter the paradise of God.

Eternal rest grant unto them, O Lord, and let perpetual light shine upon them. May they rest in peace. Amen.

Evidence of Christians

*Devout men buried Stephen, and made great
lamentation over him.* — Acts 8:2

"The teaching of the Fathers, and the formularies used in the Liturgy of the Church, found expression in the early Christian monuments, particularly those contained in the catacombs. On the tombs of the faithful were inscribed words of hope, words of petition for peace and for rest; and as the anniversaries came around the faithful gathered at the graves of the departed to make intercession for those who had gone before. At the bottom this is nothing else than the faith expressed by the Council of Trent, and to this faith the inscriptions in the catacombs are surely witnesses" — J. Pohle, *The Catholic Encyclopedia.*

Reflection: Do some research and note the dates that loved ones have died. Mark your calendar so you can especially pray for their souls on those days each year.

---

*Eternal rest grant unto them, O Lord, and let perpetual
light shine upon them. May they rest in peace. Amen.*

An Ocean of Love

*"The Lord your God is in your midst, a warrior who gives victory;
he will rejoice over you with gladness, he will renew you in his love;
he will exult over you with loud singing." — Zephaniah 3:17*

"Of the souls in purgatory we may reasonably believe, that despite their dread loneliness and unsharable sufferings, theirs is a love whose mystical richness and plentitude experiences not only God's justice but also his 'mercy, gentle and caressing as the touch of a mother; ardent as a kiss ... immense as an ocean.' The love experiences Love 'that pardons, heals, cherishes, elevates and promises union in heaven.' Likened unto Christ, their suffering is not merely an expiation; it is also an adoration. They offer their weakness in homage to Omnipotence, their tears to Beatitude, their poverty to Divine Plenitude, their darkness to Light, their silence to the Word, and their loneliness to the ineffable happiness of the Trinity" — Father Hubert, O.F.M. Cap., author.

Reflection: May the thought of the yearnings of the beloved souls spur us on to greater generosity.

---

*Eternal rest grant unto them, O Lord, and let perpetual
light shine upon them. May they rest in peace. Amen.*

OCTOBER 29

Forever at Your Side

"Behold, I send an angel before you, to guard you on the way and to bring you to the place which I have prepared." — Exodus 23:20

"When a soul goes down into purgatory, its guardian angel accompanies it to that prison, and then takes his place outside near the door, where he remains until the soul is entirely purified. He visits it frequently, to console it by his presence and heavenly discourse, and inspire it with courage.... It is his duty to collect the prayers and good works offered by the living, and to present them to God, who gives them back to him to apply them to the poor souls like a healing balm" — St. Frances of Rome.

Reflection: Pray: "Holy angel, witness of all my actions, purify me."

Eternal rest grant unto them, O Lord, and let perpetual light shine upon them. May they rest in peace. Amen.

Infinite Love

In this is love, not that we loved God but that he loved us. — 1 John 4:10

"God is like a millionaire who, having adopted a poor child, longs to be loved for Himself and not for His gifts; and so lavishes them silently, unobtrusively, as if He and they had nothing to do with each other. The position is as if God said to each one of us: 'You are my creature, having nothing of yourself, dependent for everything on Me. As such I lavish all good upon you, yet without taking advantage of My own riches and your poverty. There is love behind these gifts which alone I wish for you to discover. It is I who am poor, awaiting your personal love and longing for it. I have made you wealthy in love — a very millionaire in affection — able to pour it out when and where you will. I, Infinite Love, I thirst'" — Mother Mary of St. Austin, Helpers of the Holy Souls, author.

Reflection: Happy are those who do not wait for purgatory to repay the immense riches of God with the only riches in their power — the love of their whole heart, mind, soul, and strength.

Eternal rest grant unto them, O Lord, and let perpetual light shine upon them. May they rest in peace. Amen.

Cemetery Visit

*And the world passes away, and the lust of it; but he who
does the will of God abides for ever.* — *1 John 2:17*

"Before All Souls' Day, I went to the cemetery at dusk. Although it was locked, I managed to open the gate a bit and said, 'If you need something, my dear little souls, I will be glad to help you to the extent that the rule permits me.' I then heard these words, 'Do the will of God; we are happy in the measure that we have fulfilled God's will'" — St. Faustina (*Diary*, 518).

Reflection: To be holy is to do the will of God in the present moment. Conform your will to God's will for the sake of the suffering souls in purgatory.

---

*Eternal rest grant unto them, O Lord, and let perpetual
light shine upon them. May they rest in peace. Amen.*

Hope in the Lord in All Things

*Precious in the sight of the LORD is the death
of his saints.* — Psalm 116:15

"Today and tomorrow [All Saints' Day and All Souls' Day] are days of hope. Hope is a little like leaven that expands our souls. There are difficult moments in life, but with hope the soul goes forward and looks ahead to what awaits us.... Hope also purifies us, it lightens us; this purification in hope in Jesus Christ makes us go in haste, readily. Today before evening falls each one of us can think of the twilight of life: 'What will my passing away be like?' All of us will experience sundown, all of us! Do we look at it with hope? Do we look with that joy at being welcomed by the Lord?" — Pope Francis (November 1, 2013, Verano Cemetery, Rome).

Reflection: Make "Cemetery Sundays" a November pilgrimage. Visit the cemetery on Sundays during November, the Month of the Dead.

---

*Eternal rest grant unto them, O Lord, and let perpetual
light shine upon them. May they rest in peace. Amen.*

In This Hope We Were Saved

*Therefore he made atonement for the dead, that they might
be delivered from their sin.* — *2 Maccabees 12:45*

"On the day of the souls [All Souls' Day], as I was saying Mass, and already during my preparation for it, I felt a great devotion to the dead.... It was all due to a spiritual motion which moved me to compassion for the dead.... I thought of my father, my mother, and my relatives" — St. Peter Favre.

Reflection: Remember that to have compassion literally means "to suffer with."

*Eternal rest grant unto them, O Lord, and let perpetual
light shine upon them. May they rest in peace. Amen.*

United Souls

"But remember me, when it is well with you, and do me the kindness, I pray you, to make mention of me." — *Genesis 40:12*

"I will join you in offering Holy Communion for the dear departed one, so that God who is rich in mercy may give him a share in the inheritance of the saints in light" — Blessed Elizabeth of the Trinity.

Reflection: St. Maximilian Kolbe says: "If angels could be jealous of men, they would be so for one reason: Holy Communion. Every time you receive Holy Communion, receive it as if it were your first, last, and only Holy Communion."

Eternal rest grant unto them, O Lord, and let perpetual light shine upon them. May they rest in peace. Amen.

Suffering for Love for God

I will give to the LORD the thanks due to his righteousness, and I will sing praise to the name of the LORD, the Most High. — Psalm 7:17

"What exactly is the purification of souls in purgatory? It is a momentary separation from God, or more exactly, a delay in the union with God face to face. Why do we not suffer from this lack of union on earth? We are not, here on earth, in a state where it would be possible whereas death must bring this vision to us.

"What is the characteristic of the suffering in purgatory? It is a suffering of love. The time has come, and through the fault of the soul, the union is delayed. It is a fire of love which inspires the soul to hurl itself towards God, but it cannot. Its selfishness still enchains it, and it must rid itself of this selfishness before going to God. The soul must reach maturity in purgatory, which is like the cellar in which the fruit, harvested too soon, is left to ripen. It is an incubator of hope and love, where the embryo souls may develop, provided that their liberty succeeds — by even the slightest exertion — in hollowing out for itself this hole of light in which Man is placed beyond time and death" — Father Maurice Zundel, Swiss mystic, philosopher, author.

Reflection: What are the areas of selfishness in your life that distance you from God?

Eternal rest grant unto them, O Lord, and let perpetual light shine upon them. May they rest in peace. Amen.

Supernatural Charity

The people of Israel wept for Moses in the plains
of Moab thirty days. — Deuteronomy 34:8

The monks of Cluny had a tender devotion to the holy souls, offering their daily suffrages for the faithful departed. Many souls were freed from purgatory through their prayers. St. Odilo, their abbot, promoted this work of exquisite charity to such an extent that he ordered all monasteries to offer a Mass for the holy souls on November 2. All Souls' Day was instituted by the Church to honor the dead. The month of November has been dedicated to praying for the dead since the year 998.

Reflection: Today is also called the "second All Souls' Day," when Franciscans pray for all the deceased of their orders. Pray for their deceased today. What can you do to make the month of November extra special for all the holy souls?

Eternal rest grant unto them, O Lord, and let perpetual
light shine upon them. May they rest in peace. Amen.

Untapped Souls

Be faithful unto death, and I will give you the
crown of life. — Revelation 2:10

"Within institutes of consecrated life and societies of apostolic life there is a fraternal obligation to remember deceased sisters and confreres. Often spiritual obligations such as the offering of Masses and specific prayers are required of members to remember those who have passed away in God's friendship so that they might 'achieve the holiness necessary to enter the joy of heaven' (*Catechism of the Catholic Church*, n. 1030).

"The souls immediately begin their ministry of intercession on behalf of those here on earth. One specific area by intercession for deceased members is to pray for vocations. If called upon for prayer, they will pray on our behalf that many more young people might respond to Our Lord's invitation to 'come, follow Me' (cf. Luke 18:22).

"Let us never neglect to practice this spiritual work of mercy in praying for the dead, and always remember to tap into this reservoir of intercessory prayer for priestly and religious vocations" — Michael Wick, Institute on Religious Life.

Reflection: Sts. Zéllie and Louis Martin, the parents of St. Thérèse of Lisieux, prayed to the holy souls for the vocations of their children. Pray for your children and grandchildren or nieces and nephews that they may live their faith to the fullest! Entrust all children to the care of the holy souls and Blessed Zéllie and Blessed Louis. Ask the souls of deceased priests and religious to intercede for vocations.

Eternal rest grant unto them, O Lord, and let perpetual
light shine upon them. May they rest in peace. Amen.

Spiritual Wealth

*"I will sprinkle clean water upon you, and you shall be
clean from all your uncleanness." — Ezekiel 36:25*

Holy water is a sacramental to remind us of the Precious Blood of Jesus
Christ. It affords great benefits for body and soul and remits venial sin. It
keeps evil away.

It brings consolation to the souls of the departed. They may need the
sprinkling of just one drop to release them. Use it often for yourself, your
family, your friends, and the holy souls.

Reflection: Make devout use of holy water. Dip your finger into
the holy water and say: "By this holy water and by Your Precious
Blood, wash away all my sins, O Lord, bless my family, have mercy
on the dying, and relieve the souls in purgatory," and then make
the Sign of the Cross.

---

*Eternal rest grant unto them, O Lord, and let perpetual
light shine upon them. May they rest in peace. Amen.*

Nightly Pilgrimage to Purgatory

For wisdom is more mobile than any motion; because of her
pureness she pervades and penetrates all things. — *Wisdom 7:24*

St. Margaret Mary recommended the following devotion to her novices for the octave of All Souls' Day: "In union with the Divine Heart of Jesus make a short pilgrimage to purgatory at night. Offer Him your activities of the day and ask Him to apply His merits to the suffering souls. At the same time implore them to obtain for you the grace to live and die in the love and friendship of this Divine Heart. Fortunate will you be, if you succeed in obtaining deliverance for some of these imprisoned souls, for you will gain as many friends in heaven."

Reflection: Offer the Nine First Fridays (going to confession and receiving Holy Communion) in honor of and in reparation to the Sacred Heart. Include reparation (making atonement to God for the holy souls by prayer, sacrifice, and sufferings). Extraordinary graces are attached to this powerful devotion, including the grace of final repentance.

Eternal rest grant unto them, O Lord, and let perpetual
light shine upon them. May they rest in peace. Amen.

Gift of Peace from the Holy Souls

"So you have sorrow now, but I will see you again and your hearts will rejoice, and no one will take your joy from you." — John 16:22

"The person who shows love and compassion to those in any kind of affliction is blessed, not only with the virtue of good will but also with the gift of peace" — St. Leo the Great.

Reflection: Pray for the people in your life who have passed away this year.

Eternal rest grant unto them, O Lord, and let perpetual light shine upon them. May they rest in peace. Amen.

Helpers of the Holy Souls

"I know your works." — Revelation 3:8

"Several have made great sacrifices to God in order to obtain mercy for souls long ago called away from this world. We can all imitate their example. 'Oh, if it were not too late!' is the cry of many a heart tortured by anxiety regarding the fate of some loved one who died apparently out of the Church, or not in the state of grace. We answer: It is never too late. Pray, work, suffer. The Lord foresaw your efforts.

"The Lord knew what was to come, and may have given to that soul at its last hour some extraordinary graces which snatched it from destruction and placed it in safety, where your love may still reach it, your prayers relieve, your sacrifices avail" — Lady Georgiana Fullerton, French author who wrote about the Helpers of the Holy Souls Sisters.

Reflection: Remember the holy souls at the Divine Mercy Hour (3:00 p.m.). Pray the Chaplet of Divine Mercy (see page 391).

Eternal rest grant unto them, O Lord, and let perpetual light shine upon them. May they rest in peace. Amen.

NOVEMBER 11

Silence is Golden

*"He called out, 'Father Abraham, have mercy upon me, and
send Lazarus to dip the end of his finger in water and cool my
tongue; for I am in anguish in this flame.'"* — *Luke 16:24*

We are told "death and life are in the power of the tongue" (Prov 18:21).
Purgatory is filled with suffering souls who committed sins of the tongue.
St. Alphonsus Liguori wrote: "Oh, how great the blessings that silence
brings to the soul! The prophet [Isaiah] says that silence shall cultivate
justice in the souls [Is 32:17]; for, on the one hand, it saves us from a multitude of sins by destroying the root of disputes, of detractions, of resent-
ments, and of curiosity; and on the other hand, it makes us acquire many
virtues." The same holy prophet said: "In quietness and in trust shall be
your strength" (Is 30:15).

Reflection: Consciously tame your tongue today. In the spirit of
reparation, keep a day of silence to bring solace to the suffering
souls.

---

*Eternal rest grant unto them, O Lord, and let perpetual
light shine upon them. May they rest in peace. Amen.*

"St. Dearly Departed"

*"O death, where is thy victory? O death,
where is thy sting"? — 1 Corinthians 15:55*

"We forget the duty of a priest at a funeral Mass is not to make people 'feel good' by telling them that Aunt Flo or Uncle Bob is now in heaven with the Father; instead he is to offer worship to God for Christ's Victory over death, to comfort the mourning with prayers and the Eucharist and to pray for the souls of the deceased — commending the souls to God's merciful love. To presume the deceased is in heaven is to presume the mind of God. Of course, we can go straight to heaven. But let's face it, most of us won't" — Peggy Frye, convert from an evangelical church, Catholic apologist.

Reflection: Remember with gratitude those who set a good example for you. Be an example to others.

---

*Eternal rest grant unto them, O Lord, and let perpetual
light shine upon them. May they rest in peace. Amen.*

Save Souls

To him who loves us and has freed us from our sins by his blood ... to him be glory and dominion for ever and ever. — Revelation 1:6

"Suddenly a choir of souls already saved woke her up. They showed how they had just left purgatory. They looked as glorious and joyful as one can think of. They then spoke lovingly to Margaret [of Cortona], and greeting her they were raised up high to land in paradise in the bosom of God. Most joyful ascension! Afterwards, often other souls would appear to her very sad, begging her to show mercy to them also. Margaret would add more prayers, and the following day she would receive Communion. What a joy! And so more souls rose up on high exclaiming: 'Holy Communion saves souls, Holy Communion saves souls!'" — St. Louis Guanella, founder of the Pious Union of St. Joseph in 1924.

Reflection: Pray this prayer throughout the day: "Jesus, Mary, and Joseph, I love you, save souls!"

Eternal rest grant unto them, O Lord, and let perpetual light shine upon them. May they rest in peace. Amen.

Seeing for the First Time

For we walk by faith, not by sight. — *2 Corinthians 5:6*

"Might purgatory be understood precisely as being embraced by God in such a way that this warmth and light so dwarf our earthly concepts of love and knowledge that, like a person born blind who is given sight, we have to struggle painfully in the very ecstasy of that light to unlearn and relearn virtually our entire way of thinking and loving? Might purgatory be understood not as God's absence or some kind of punishment or retribution for sin, but as what happens to us when we are fully embraced, in ecstasy, by God, perfect love and perfect truth? Indeed, isn't this what faith, hope, and charity, the three cardinal virtues, are already trying to move us toward in this life? Isn't faith a knowing beyond what we can conceptualize? Isn't hope an anchoring of ourselves in something beyond what we can control and guarantee for ourselves? And isn't charity reaching out beyond what affectively feeds us?" — Father Ronald Rolheiser, O.M.I., author.

Reflection: Ask Jesus to show you the sins you are too blind to see. Confession is the remedy.

Eternal rest grant unto them, O Lord, and let perpetual light shine upon them. May they rest in peace. Amen.

Graces beyond Belief

*"The LORD recompense you for what you have done, and a full
reward be given you by the LORD, the God of Israel, under
whose wings you have come to take refuge!"* — Ruth 2:12

"These glorious souls know that the good they receive from us is infinite and being most grateful they show their gratitude proportionate to the greatness of their enjoyment. We will have so many intercessors in the courts of Heaven to look after us" — Mother Mary of St. Austin, Helpers of the Holy Souls, author.

Reflection: With holy boldness intercede for the release of all souls in purgatory, who will be eternally grateful.

---

*Eternal rest grant unto them, O Lord, and let perpetual
light shine upon them. May they rest in peace. Amen.*

NOVEMBER 16

Anchored in Charity

*"When he ascended on high he led a host of captives,
and he gave gifts to men." — Ephesians 4:8*

"On Wednesday, at the elevation of the Host, I besought Our Lord for the souls of the faithful in purgatory, that He would free them from their pains by virtue of His admirable Ascension; and I beheld Our Lord descending into purgatory with a gold rod in His Hand, which has as many hooks as there had been prayers for their souls; by these He appeared to draw them into a place of repose. I understood by this, that whenever anyone prays generally, from a motive of charity, for the souls in purgatory, the greatest part of those who, during their lives, have exercised themselves in works of charity, are released" — St. Gertrude.

Reflection: Say the Eternal Rest Prayer (see below) for those souls you hear about in the news, read about online, or learn about in the newspaper.

---

*Eternal rest grant unto them, O Lord, and let perpetual
light shine upon them. May they rest in peace. Amen.*

Stages of a Soul's Life

So we, though many, are one body in Christ, and
individually members one of another. — *Romans 12:5*

"One evening one of the deceased sisters, who had already visited me a few times, appeared to me. The first time I had seen her, she had been in great suffering, and then gradually these sufferings had diminished; this time she was radiant with happiness, and she told me she was already in heaven.... And further as a sign that she only now was in heaven, God would bless our house. Then she came closer to me, embraced me sincerely and said, 'I must go now.' I understood how closely the three stages of a soul's life are bound together; that is to say, life on earth, in purgatory and in heaven [the Communion of Saints]" — St. Faustina (*Diary*, 594).

Reflection: Offer a special prayer for a deceased religious whom you knew while growing up.

Eternal rest grant unto them, O Lord, and let perpetual
light shine upon them. May they rest in peace. Amen.

The Need for Purgatory

God will bring every deed into judgment, with every
secret thing, whether good or evil. — Ecclesiastes 12:14

"I would go so far as to say that if there was no purgatory, then we would have to invent it, for who would dare say of himself that he was able to stand directly before God?

"And yet we don't want to be, to use an image from Scripture, 'a pot that turned out wrong,' that has to be thrown away; we want to be put right. Purgatory basically means that God can put the pieces back together again. That he can cleanse us in such a way that we are able to be with him and can stand there in the fullness of life" — Joseph Cardinal Ratzinger (Pope Benedict XVI).

Reflection: Ask the Lord to cleanse your soul so that you can put back together the broken pieces of your life.

Eternal rest grant unto them, O Lord, and let perpetual
light shine upon them. May they rest in peace. Amen.

Attaining Heaven without Delay

*The sacrifice acceptable to God is a broken spirit; a broken
contrite heart, O God, thou will not despise.* — Psalm 51:17

"Marie of St. Joseph, a pillar of the Teresian Reform, was favored by God
with an earthly purgatory, in the form of great sufferings during the last
years of her life.

"Left without speech and with terrible suffering, the hearts were broken of her sisters who assisted by her side. One of them whispered to her
to make an act of resignation to the will of God. She did and kept doing
so until she died. God revealed to the sister (Isabella) who directed her to
do this, that she had passed directly to Heaven. The deceased sister also
appeared to her and thanked her for suggesting those acts of resignation
which had merited for her a great reward in Heaven and avoiding purgatory altogether" — St. Teresa of Ávila, on the death of a sister.

Reflection: Open your heart and soul to the will of God and trust in
His goodness. Give thanks and praise for the greatness and beauty
of the life He gives you.

---

*Eternal rest grant unto them, O Lord, and let perpetual
light shine upon them. May they rest in peace. Amen.*

Words of Wisdom from a Soul

*Put on then, as God's chosen ones, holy and beloved, compassion,
kindness, lowliness, meekness, and patience. — Proverbs 11:17*

" 'Be good, be good for people! Be good, think good, speak good, do good! Up there, there is only love!' A purgatorial soul needing the sacrifice of being good. He did not give love during his life" — Father Hermann Wagner, German author.

Reflection: Be kind to someone who is difficult to deal with out of love for the saintly sufferers.

*Eternal rest grant unto them, O Lord, and let perpetual
light shine upon them. May they rest in peace. Amen.*

Making Up

*"For if you forgive men their trespasses, your heavenly
Father also will forgive you." — Matthew 6:13*

"Prayers for the dead also express our belief that our prayers can help those who have gone before us in death. Forgiveness of sin is given in this life; but making up for sin is, at least in part, often done in the next. We all know that asking for and accepting forgiveness isn't always enough to repair a relationship. 'How can I make it up to you?' we ask people we have harmed. Acts of love and penance strengthen our relationships to one another and to God. 'Making up' for the consequences of sin, the sins of those in purgatory and our own, is a project the Church bids us take to heart this month" — Francis Cardinal George, O.M.I.

Reflection: Pope Francis reminds us to say: "May I?" "Thank you." "I am sorry." " Excuse me." Pray the Prayer of Daily Neglects (see page 394). A soul avoided purgatory by means of this prayer.

---

*Eternal rest grant unto them, O Lord, and let perpetual
light shine upon them. May they rest in peace. Amen.*

Blessed Ones Cry Out

*Give heed to my groaning. Hearken to
the sound of my cry.* — Psalm 5:1-2

"If a ray of heavenly light could draw aside the veil from your eyes, you
would see these suffering souls hovering around each station with upraised
arms imploring you, 'Have pity on me, have pity on me!' In pity for us,
make the Way of the Cross for me, your father, your mother, your friend"
— St. Leonard of Port Maurice.

Reflection: Pray the Way of the Cross on Fridays at home or in
church for the anxious souls in purgatory. If we could see them, we
would reach out!

---

*Eternal rest grant unto them, O Lord, and let perpetual
light shine upon them. May they rest in peace. Amen.*

Putting Your Soul in Order

"Unless one is born anew, he cannot see the kingdom of God." — John 3:3

"Everything unclean must go. Everything twisted and bent as a result of sin must be straightened out. Everything crippled and sick in the depths of our soul must be healed, and everything out of its proper order must be put into order. Every attachment that is not to the Lord and in the Lord must be broken. The illness we suffer from is grave and life threatening; the medicine to cure this 'sickness unto death' must itself be very strong to be effective" — Ralph Martin, president of Renewal Ministries, professor, author.

Reflection: Make an appointment with the Divine Physician and make a holy hour in reparation before the Blessed Sacrament for our holy heroes.

Eternal rest grant unto them, O Lord, and let perpetual light shine upon them. May they rest in peace. Amen.

Love Lasts Forever

I looked for pity, but there was none; and for comforters, but I found none. — Psalm 69:20

"Praying for one's departed loved ones is a far too immediate urge to be suppressed; it is a most beautiful manifestation of solidarity, love and assistance, reaching beyond the barrier of death. The happiness or unhappiness of a person dear to me, who has now crossed to the other shore, depends in part on whether I remember or forget him; he does not stop needing my love" — Joseph Cardinal Ratzinger (Pope Benedict XVI).

Reflection: Whenever a memory of a loved one or a name arises, offer a prayer for the repose of that person's soul.

Eternal rest grant unto them, O Lord, and let perpetual light shine upon them. May they rest in peace. Amen.

Unlock Purgatory

*And though the betrothed young woman cried for help there
was no one to rescue her. — Deuteronomy 22:27*

"God has given the keys of purgatory to us, but not to them" — Blessed
James Alberione, Italian priest, founder of the Daughters of St. Paul and
the Society of St. Paul, author.

Reflection: The souls in purgatory cannot help themselves. Their
time of merit is up. They are helpless. They cry out, "God, God,
I must be with God!" We alone are their only resource. We are
given the duty, power, and privilege to deliver them. We have an
obligation to pray for our deceased loved ones. Our responsibility
is great. God's justice demands expiation (penance) of their sins.
He places in our hands the means to assist them. Unlock the door
to heaven for the souls with Holy Mass, the Rosary, the Way of
the Cross for the Holy Souls in Purgatory, Eucharistic adoration.
These are the "pillars" of prayer to relieve and release the suffering
souls in purgatory. Remember in a special way those souls who
died a violent death.

---

*Eternal rest grant unto them, O Lord, and let perpetual
light shine upon them. May they rest in peace. Amen.*

For the Glory of God

*And I heard a voice from heaven saying, "Write this: Blessed
are the dead who die in the Lord henceforth." "Blessed
indeed," says the Spirit, "that they may rest from their labors,
for their deeds follow them!" — Revelation 14:13*

"Because our works *do* follow us, and not all of them are good works, or
even if they are good, they are full of faults and imperfections, it is necessary for the soul to be purified of every blemish before being admitted to
the vision of God. And yet, if we were perfectly faithful to grace, there
would be no need of purgatory, for God purifies here below those who give
themselves wholly to Him, who let themselves be fashioned and formed
according to His good pleasure. Furthermore, purification accomplished
on earth has the great advantage of being meritorious, that is, of increas-
ing grace and charity in us, thus permitting us to love God more for all
eternity; whereas in purgatory, one suffers without growing in charity.
That is why we should desire to be purified during life" — Father Gabriel
of St. Mary Magdalen, O.C.D., lecturer, author.

Reflection: May the thought of that place of expiation rouse our zeal
to pray for the souls of the departed, and may it also make us more
courageous in embracing suffering in reparation for our own faults.
Recite this spiritual aspiration: "For the greater glory of God, I beg
you to cleanse a soul in most need for your mercy and forgiveness."

---

*Eternal rest grant unto them, O Lord, and let perpetual
light shine upon them. May they rest in peace. Amen.*

Our Need for Cleansing

*Beloved, do not be surprised at the fiery ordeal which
comes upon you to prove you, as though something
strange were happening to you. — 1 Peter 4:12*

"Do not care for the present, as many have done, only to find themselves
deceived at last; but lift your eyes to heaven, for which you were created,
and pray that you may be there, be the cost what it may. None of those
who are already there have passed through the world without greater afflictions than you have; if some of them had less to bear their tortures were
incomparably more severe in purgatory, for Our Lord has ordained that
none shall take part in his joys but they who have shared his pains. He has
kept this rule with all souls beloved by him, therefore let us not complain
of it nor feel aggrieved, even if we had the option of passing through life
without sharing in the pains he and his Mother bore. This is the road to
heaven, let us walk in it; it is the purgatory of our sins, do not let us think
it too hard"— St. John of Ávila.

Reflection: In planning a trip or vacation, we carefully work out all
the details. Do we do the same in regards to our eternal destina-
tion?

---

*Eternal rest grant unto them, O Lord, and let perpetual
light shine upon them. May they rest in peace. Amen.*

Work While It Is Still Day

Whatever your task, work heartily, as serving the Lord, and not men, knowing that from the Lord you will receive the inheritance as your reward. — Colossians 3:23-24

"For the poor souls their work does not count. It is penal labor, a wearing out of one's self without any effect. Their efforts obtain nothing; it flows, yet dries up as a river in the sand. Thank God for us the bright light of day is still shining; it is still time when we can work, when nothing is done in vain. Everything we do while it is still day. We can offer the Holy Mass, we can suffer, we can give them the fruit of your prayers. Give them the merits of your good works. Give and it shall be given to you!" — Paul von Keppler, bishop (of Rottenburg, Germany), author.

Reflection: When you make your Morning Offering remember to include your thoughts, words, and actions for the suffering souls (see page 392).

Eternal rest grant unto them, O Lord, and let perpetual light shine upon them. May they rest in peace. Amen.

Treasures for Your Soul

"And as you wish that men would do to you, do so to them." — *Luke 6:31*

"Do you think then it is suitable to plead on behalf of the souls in purgatory? Let us pray for them more heartily. We offer poor gifts for them from our heart. Those blessed souls obtain for us abundant treasures from heaven. He who offers a prayer for the souls in purgatory obtains a treasure for his own soul" — St. Louis Guanella, founder of the Pious Union of St. Joseph in 1924.

Reflection: Next time you look at your bank account balance, ask yourself if you show the same abundance of treasures for the suffering souls in purgatory.

Eternal rest grant unto them, O Lord, and let perpetual light shine upon them. May they rest in peace. Amen.

What's in It for You?

I will thank thee for ever, because thou hast done it. — Psalm 52:9

"When judgment day dawns, a chorus of voices will rise in our behalf, for those liberated souls will cry out: 'This priest, these sisters, this child, this man, this woman helped us and freed us. We were in purgatory and you descended among us to extinguish the flames. You comforted us and your suffrages opened the way to heaven.' And Jesus will say to you: 'Yes, I remember it now and I will remember it for all eternity. The Holy Spirit which I gave you did not return to me. The seed that was planted has borne fruit. You showed mercy and mercy shall be yours. Blessed are the merciful for they shall receive mercy. Come, blessed of my Father, take possession of the kingdom prepared for you from the foundation of the world'" — Paul von Keppler, bishop (of Rottenburg, Germany), author.

Reflection: Spend some time today imagining your own day of judgment. Will the holy souls testify on your behalf?

Eternal rest grant unto them, O Lord, and let perpetual light shine upon them. May they rest in peace. Amen.

DECEMBER 1

Good Angels

One thing have I asked of the LORD, that will I seek after;
that I may dwell in the house of the LORD all the days of my
life, to behold the beauty of the LORD. — Psalm 27:4

"Those dear friends for whom I mourn have only passed away from my sight for a little while, and I shall soon rejoin them; in the meantime, they think of me, and are interested in all that concerns me. They know, through their good angels and my own, all that I wish to tell them, all that I do for them; they watch over me, they follow and protect me in all the dangers and trials of life" — Blessed Frédéric Ozanam.

Reflection: Pray the Guardian Angel Prayer with the piety of an angel (see page 391).

Eternal rest grant unto them, O Lord, and let perpetual
light shine upon them. May they rest in peace. Amen.

Plea for Neglected Souls

*"Is it nothing to you, all you who pass by? Look and
see if there is any sorrow like my sorrow which was
brought upon me." — Lamentations 1:12*

"Remember our thirst while you sit and drink, our hunger while you are feasting, our restless watch while you are sleeping, our sore and grievous pain while you are playing, our hot burning fire while you are in pleasure and sporting. So may God make your offspring ... remember you, so God keep you away or not long here, but bring you shortly to that bliss, to which, for our Lord's love, you help to bring us and we shall set hand to help you there" — St. Thomas More in reply to the attacks against Masses for the dead.

Reflection: Fast today in some way in reparation for the souls of those who committed suicide.

*Eternal rest grant unto them, O Lord, and let perpetual
light shine upon them. May they rest in peace. Amen.*

Faith in Purgatory

As his majesty is, so also is his mercy. — Sirach 2:18

"The doctrine of purgatory is one of wisdom and consolation. It emphasizes the sanctity and majesty of God, since nothing soiled can appear before Him. It fortifies our sense of justice. It manifests the disorder, often unperceived, of venial faults.

"Faith in purgatory purifies us here on earth" — Father Reginald Garrigou-Lagrange, O.P., French theologian, author.

Reflection: Dive into the *Catechism of the Catholic Church* on purgatory with your family. Especially read paragraphs 1030-1032.

---

*Eternal rest grant unto them, O Lord, and let perpetual
light shine upon them. May they rest in peace. Amen.*

DECEMBER 4

The Hidden Face of God

We all, with unveiled face, beholding the glory of
the Lord, are being changed into his likeness from one
degree of glory to another. — 2 Corinthians 3:18

"In purgatory the Holy Spirit is the Breath of God who has made each of its inhabitants lovable to its Spouse. He is the loving, tranquil, sweet Ravisher of each holy soul. He floods the still amazement of its night with a mysterious foretaste of the ineffable God. He increases its love-longing for the blessed vision of peace until it becomes nearly unendurable. And yet He acts in each soul with love's most tender vengeance, close-veiling the vision of God until it has fully matured to the level of the growth in grace during the day of this life" — Karl Rahner, S.J., German theologian, author.

Reflection: Implore the Holy Spirit to breathe a renewed sense of the sacred within your soul.

Eternal rest grant unto them, O Lord, and let perpetual
light shine upon them. May they rest in peace. Amen.

Arms Wide Open

O give thanks to the LORD, for he is good; his steadfast love endures forever! / Let Israel say, "His steadfast love endures forever." / Let the House of Aaron say, "His steadfast love endures forever." / Let those who fear the LORD say, "His steadfast love endures forever." — Psalm 118:2-4

"As for Paradise, God has placed no doors there. Whoever wishes to enter, does so.

"All-merciful God stands there with his arms open, waiting to receive us into his glory. I also see, however, that the divine essence is so pure and light-filled — much more than we can imagine — that the soul that has but the slightest imperfection would rather throw itself into a thousand hells than appear before his infinite holiness. The soul gladly plunges itself in purgatory with happiness and accepts with gratitude as a proof of God's infinite mercy the means of removing the stain of sin which prevents it from being united with the only object of its love" — St. Catherine of Genoa.

Reflection: Ponder the incredible holiness and mercy of God.

Eternal rest grant unto them, O Lord, and let perpetual light shine upon them. May they rest in peace. Amen.

Love Is All There Is

"I have loved you with an everlasting love." — *Jeremiah 31:3*

"As I was praying to our Lord for the dear souls in purgatory and asking him to make me know something of the relations which exist between him and them, he answered me: 'Between Love and love there is nothing but love.' And a vivid and gentle light disclosed to me the extreme suffering of those souls dominated and absorbed by divine love" — Lucie Christine, French mystic, author.

Reflection: Pray that you can be the grace that helps the holy souls be absorbed into the divine love of God.

Eternal rest grant unto them, O Lord, and let perpetual light shine upon them. May they rest in peace. Amen.

DECEMBER 7

Escorts to Heavens

*I was glad when they said to me, "Let us go
to the house of the LORD!"* — Psalm 122:1

St. John Macias worked for the sick in Peru and, no matter how tired he was, prayed three Rosaries on his knees every night for the poor souls in purgatory. On his deathbed, St. John the Evangelist appeared to him and said that through his prayers St. John Macias had released one million four hundred thousand souls from purgatory. When he died, thousands upon thousands of souls poured from heaven to greet him.

Reflection: Appeal to the holy souls to be with you at the hour of your death.

---

*Eternal rest grant unto them, O Lord, and let perpetual
light shine upon them. May they rest in peace. Amen.*

O Immaculata, Be Present to Us!

*"I am the handmaid of the Lord, let it be done to
me according to your word."* — Luke 1:38

Blessed Paul VI called the Marian sanctuaries — Lourdes, Fátima, Guadalupe — "spiritual clinics." We bring our ailments: living without God as the center of our lives, lack of mercy and compassion, lack of appreciation of the gift of life. All weaken our souls. Powerful conversions occur at these shrines through God's grace and the maternal intercession of the Mother of God. Healings take place by God through His Word. "Patients" encounter Jesus in the sacrament of reconciliation and the Holy Eucharist. Visit these privileged places to encounter Christ and rediscover your sense of baptismal vocation and to hear its saving call.

Reflection: Visit a shrine or church dedicated to Mary. Deepen your love for Mary Immaculate, so that her maternal embrace may greet you upon your death. Join with St. Bonaventure in praying: "I ask Thee, O Mary, for the glory of Thy name, to come and meet my soul when it is departing from this world, and to take it in your arms."

---

*Eternal rest grant unto them, O Lord, and let perpetual
light shine upon them. May they rest in peace. Amen.*

DECEMBER 9

To the Ones We Love

Finally, all of you, have unity of spirit, sympathy, love of the brethren, a tender heart and a humble mind. — 1 Peter 3:8

"We did not tell them we loved them as much as we could have, or maybe we hurt them by not fully forgiving them for some wrong. Purgatory, then, enables us to atone for our ingratitude because through our prayers, mortifications, and sacrifices, it makes it possible to bring joy and consolation to the ones we love" — Venerable Archbishop Fulton J. Sheen.

Reflection: Be one with the holy souls in their love, their eager expectation, and their union with God.

Eternal rest grant unto them, O Lord, and let perpetual light shine upon them. May they rest in peace. Amen.

Soul Virtues

*So faith, hope, love abide, these three; but the greatest
of these is love.* — *1 Corinthians 13:13*

"In Christ we were to find the model of how to live human life correctly. We were to be like him — a person who lived completely for others, who loved and served selflessly. More than all else, Jesus wanted his followers to be people of faith, hope, and love. These soul-virtues not only identified us as his disciples; they were the means that best prepared us for our life with him in heaven. Faith brings us to Jesus, hope keeps us there, and selfless love refashions us in his image. Heaven is for Christ-like people. This is what God will be looking for" — Father Michael J. Taylor, S.J., Scripture scholar, author.

Reflection: When people look at you do they see a reflection of Jesus?

*Eternal rest grant unto them, O Lord, and let perpetual
light shine upon them. May they rest in peace. Amen.*

Message from the Holy Souls

*Let us not grow weary in well-doing, for in due season we
shall reap, if we do not lose heart. — Galatians 6:9*

"Bring them a greeting from us, they say, preach to them and touch their conscience. Tell them to work while it is still day. Tell them to make good use of their time and perform the work and mission that has been given to them by God so you may weave gold threads of good works, of sacraments received, of charity given, of Sundays kept holy into the tissue of their lives. Tell them that often the day suddenly changes into night when no man can work; that perhaps many of those who are alive today will not be here next year! Have we forgotten? Do we have time for them to reach the throne of God?" — Paul von Keppler, bishop (of Rottenburg, Germany), author.

Reflection: Do you utilize your time each day in light of eternity?

---

*Eternal rest grant unto them, O Lord, and let perpetual
light shine upon them. May they rest in peace. Amen.*

Do Not Be Sad

*"Blessed are those who mourn, for they shall
be comforted." — Matthew 5:4*

"Any good Christian should be busy trying to give comfort to the suffering. How about your own family and friends who have gone before you? Follow St. Monica's advice: Pray for them at the altar of God. And don't be sad about it all. The Venerable Henry Newman wrote a marvelous poem, 'The Dream of Gerontius,' in which he applies St. Catherine of Genoa's teaching to the experience of an old man from the moment of death until his entrance into purgatory. His Guardian Angel accompanies him, and as he enters into the purifying bath of purgatory, the angel says to him: 'Farewell, but not forever! Brother dear, / Be brave and patient on thy bed of sorrow; / Swiftly shall pass thy night of trial here, / And I will come and wake thee on the morrow.' " — Father Benedict Groeschel, C.F.R., psychologist, author.

Reflection: For the gracious souls, offer to God your spiritual and corporal works of mercy done for the living.

---

*Eternal rest grant unto them, O Lord, and let perpetual
light shine upon them. May they rest in peace. Amen.*

Sacrifice and Consolation

*He who has a bountiful eye will be blessed, for he shares
his bread with the poor. — Proverbs 22:9*

"Weep for those who die in their wealth and who with all their wealth prepared no consolation for their own souls, who had the power to wash away their sins and did not will to do it. Let us weep for them, let us assist them to the extent of our ability, let us think of some assistance for them, small as it may be, yet let us somehow assist them. But how, and in what way? By praying for them and by entreating others to pray for them, by constantly giving alms to the poor on their behalf. Not in vain was it decreed by the apostles that in the awesome mysteries, remembrance should be made of the departed. They knew that here there was much gain for them, much benefit, when the entire people stands with hands uplifted, a priestly assembly, and that awesome sacrificial Victim is laid out, how, when we are calling upon God, should we not succeed in their defense? But this is done for those who have departed in the faith while even the catechumens are not reckoned as worthy of this consolation, but are deprived of every means of assistance except one. And what is that? We may give alms to the poor on their behalf" — St. John Chrysostom.

Reflection: Do we share with the poor from our abundance or from our need? The poor will open the gates of heaven for you!

---

*Eternal rest grant unto them, O Lord, and let perpetual
light shine upon them. May they rest in peace. Amen.*

God's Will in All

"I have come to do thy will, O God." — *Hebrews 10:7*

"In the evening when I was walking in the garden saying my rosary and came to the cemetery, I opened the gate a little and began to pray for a while, and I asked them interiorly, 'You are very happy are you not?' Then I heard the words, 'We are happy in the measure that we have fulfilled God's will' — and then silence as before. I became introspective and reflected for a long time on how I am fulfilling God's will and how I am profiting from the time that God has given me" — St. Faustina (*Diary*, 515).

Reflection: Those who do God's will lose nothing. They find the real treasure that gives meaning to all things. This is the secret to true joy in God. Take a drive through a cemetery and pray for all the deceased souls who rest there.

---

*Eternal rest grant unto them, O Lord, and let perpetual
light shine upon them. May they rest in peace. Amen.*

Longing for God in Suffering

May mercy, peace, and love be multiplied to you. — Jude 1:2

"Place on one side, only the pain of loss; place on the other a hundred fires of hell; know that the one alone is greater than the hundred. Those souls, while they are isolated from God, feel an inexpressible love toward their infinitely good Father — a consuming desire to rush toward him, the God of consolation!" — St. John Chrysostom.

Reflection: Pray the Lord's Prayer slowly and devoutly in honor of the holy souls.

Eternal rest grant unto them, O Lord, and let perpetual light shine upon them. May they rest in peace. Amen.

Unfathomable, Inexhaustible Mercy

*Do you not know that God's kindness is meant to
lead you to repentance?* — Romans 2:4

"O Jesus, I understand that Your mercy is beyond all imagining, and therefore, I ask You to make my heart so big that there will be room in it for the needs of all the souls living on the face of the earth. O Jesus, my love extends beyond the world, to the souls suffering in purgatory, and I want to exercise mercy toward them by means of indulgenced prayers. God's mercy is unfathomable and inexhaustible, just as God Himself is unfathomable. Even if I were to use the strongest words there are to express this mercy of God, all this would be nothing in comparison with what it is in reality. O Jesus, make my heart sensitive to all the sufferings of my neighbor, whether of body or of soul. O my Jesus, I know that You act toward us as we act toward our neighbor. My Jesus, make my heart like unto Your merciful Heart. Jesus, help me to go through life doing good to everyone" — St. Faustina (*Diary*, 692).

Reflection: O Jesus, liberate the souls who are so dear to you.

---

*Eternal rest grant unto them, O Lord, and let perpetual
light shine upon them. May they rest in peace. Amen.*

One with the Most Abandoned

*And when the chief Shepherd is manifested you will
obtain the unfading crown of glory.* — 1 Peter 5:4

"When we think of the aloneness of Jesus, it is impossible to say of a fellow sinner, 'Well, he has driven everyone away, and now suffers what he deserves.' We are not permitted to speak in that fashion. It may be that in the sinner's destitution he is drawing close to the heart of Jesus, whose hand even now may be resting upon that lost sheep's shoulder. Likewise, the least of souls in purgatory enjoys an incomparable gift which we do not yet enjoy. He, despite his suffering and also in and through his suffering, is already among the saved, and God's grace protects him from committing a single sin, while we can hardly endure a day without indulging our pride, or falling back into sloth and cowardice. Sheep indeed.

"But to pray for the souls in purgatory, is like playing a prelude which begins in darkness and moves always toward light and joy. It is a wonderful thing to know that the most abandoned among us, through the blood of Christ, will stand at the doorway to paradise, no less than the greatest of saints will have done before" — Anthony Esolen, professor, author.

Reflection: Know that you are never alone if you remember the holy souls. Remember those who do not believe in the doctrine of purgatory.

---

*Eternal rest grant unto them, O Lord, and let perpetual
light shine upon them. May they rest in peace. Amen.*

Only the Pure Enter Heaven

When shall I come and behold the face of God? — Psalm 42:2

St. Augustine, St. Gregory, and St. Caesarius of Arles agreed: Purgatory will be terminated for everyone at the time of the final general judgment of humanity. It ends for an individual when he or she has been purified to be able to enter into heaven. The elect will find before dying, sufficient purification.

Reflection: The perfection of heaven allows entrance of only those who have been made pure. Beg God's forgiveness for any sins that would prevent you from entering heaven.

Eternal rest grant unto them, O Lord, and let perpetual light shine upon them. May they rest in peace. Amen.

Keep Your Focus on Eternity

Seek the LORD and his strength, seek
his presence continually! — Psalm 105:4

"It is a serious mistake to have purgatory as a goal. Paradise is our goal and purgatory is a sign of the mercy of God, a sign that we have ignored His assistance while on earth but are still in His care" — Blessed James Alberione, Italian priest, founder of the Daughters of St. Paul and the Society of St. Paul, author.

Reflection: Always aim high ... do not settle!

Eternal rest grant unto them, O Lord, and let perpetual
light shine upon them. May they rest in peace. Amen.

The Divine Work of Purgatory

"There is none holy like the Lord, there is none besides thee;
there is no rock like our God." — 1 Samuel 2:2

"The holy souls are cleansed by the attributes of God. In heaven, God's attribute — his glory, his power, his sanctity, his truth, his wisdom, his beatitude — will be shared with us in greater measure than any of God's gifts on earth. For the *Justice of God* will be our glittering raiment; *infinite Holiness* will be the breath of our being; the *Ineffable* God will be our ineffable beatitude; the *Immensity* of God will be our solitude; the *Silence of God* our rest, the overflowing source of perfect life, praise, activity. The *Being* of God by whom we are possessed will be our possession; the *Beauty of God* the repose of our vision; the *Father*, the *Son*, the *Holy Spirit*, our source of expression and communication of life everlasting; and the *Unity of the Triune God* will be our selfless joy, one with all others for evermore" — Mother Mary of St. Austin, Helpers of the Holy Souls, author.

Reflection: The purgations of purgatory are the heavenly remedies through which is attained rest and life everlasting, and a rejoicing in the glory of heaven forever.

Eternal rest grant unto them, O Lord, and let perpetual
light shine upon them. May they rest in peace. Amen.

Teach the Children

*"Unless you turn and become like children, you will never
enter the kingdom of heaven." — Matthew 18:3*

"[French scholar] John Gerson took great pains to teach the children
to repeat often these words: 'My God, my Creator, have pity on your
poor servant, John Gerson.' For these innocent souls, all the while the
good man was dying, and after his death, ... went up and down the town
with a mournful voice, singing the short lesson he had taught them, and
comforting his soul with their innocent prayers" — Eitienne Binet, S.J.,
French author.

Reflection: Teach the children to never let go of Our Lady's hand.
That is, hang on to her Rosary! Pray often: "My God, my Creator,
have pity on your poor servant."

---

*Eternal rest grant unto them, O Lord, and let perpetual
light shine upon them. May they rest in peace. Amen.*

God's Flames of Love

Thy word is a lamp to my feet and a light to my path. — *Psalm 119:105*

St. John of the Cross described the purification of the spirit as "a living flame of love that tenderly wounds my soul in its deepest center." He added: "This dark night is an inflow of God into the soul, which purges it of its habitual ignorances and imperfections, natural and spiritual.... Through this contemplation, God teaches the soul secretly and instructs it in the perfection of love without its doing anything, nor understanding how this happens.... There are two reasons why this divine wisdom is not only night and darkness for the soul, but also affliction and torment. First, because of the height of the divine wisdom which exceeds the capacity of the soul. Second, because of the soul's baseness and impurity; and on this account it is painful, afflictive, and also dark for the soul."

Reflection: Be fervent in spreading acts of kindness throughout the day for these pain-stricken souls. You will receive a copious increase of grace.

*Eternal rest grant unto them, O Lord, and let perpetual
light shine upon them. May they rest in peace. Amen.*

Everlasting Now

*"Her sins, which are many, are forgiven,
for she loved much." — Luke 7:47*

"Be charitable to others, and they will be no less to you. The time is not long that is allowed you to sojourn in this world; in this little time, be sure you make the Saints in heaven and the souls in purgatory your friends; that they be obliged to help you in your greatest need. Learn to have a tender heart for the poor souls, and to use your utmost endeavors to go directly into heaven" — Salvian, fifth-century Christian writer.

Reflection: Pray for those who are slaves to sin that they might be unshackled.

---

*Eternal rest grant unto them, O Lord, and let perpetual
light shine upon them. May they rest in peace. Amen.*

Deliver Them, O Lord!

*"Men will come from east and west, and from north and south,
and sit at table in the kingdom of God." — Luke 13:29*

"Most souls are released on Christmas Day. Followed by Easter, then Our Lord's feast days, and Our Lady's feast days and Saturdays as days of rest, consolation and deliverance" — St. Alphonsus Liguori.

Reflection: To best celebrate Christmas, let's deck heaven's halls with the holy souls this holy, holiday season!

*Eternal rest grant unto them, O Lord, and let perpetual
light shine upon them. May they rest in peace. Amen.*

Christmas in Paradise

The people who walked in darkness have seen a great light; for us a child is born, and his name will be called "Wonderful Counselor, Mighty God, Everlasting Father, Prince of Peace." — Isaiah 9:2, 6

St. Faustina's request on the day of her perpetual vows:

"Jesus, I plead with You for the souls that are most in need of prayer. I plead for the dying; be merciful to them. I also beg You, Jesus, to free all souls from purgatory" (*Diary*, 240).

Reflection: Join St. Faustina in begging Jesus to empty purgatory. Offer your Mass, Holy Communion, and indulgences for their release. Remember, heaven encourages them, you deliver them. Fall in adoration like the shepherds at the manger. Love Jesus, adore Him, thank Him, sing praises to Jesus for His birthday and for the holy souls' birth into heaven.

Eternal rest grant unto them, O Lord, and let perpetual light shine upon them. May they rest in peace. Amen.

The Mystical Body of Christ

The tombs also were opened, and many bodies of the saints who had fallen asleep were raised, and coming out of the tombs after his resurrection they went into the holy city and appeared to many. — Matthew 27:52-53

Early Christians chose their resting places near the tombs of the martyrs. Why? Intercessory prayer. Christians carved inscriptions and supplications on loved ones' tombs, seeking prayers for their dead. They revealed a certain conviction that union with God (after death) has been delayed by the remnants of sin. Prayer for the dead includes the confidence and hope that God will purify them according to their need. The purpose of burial near the tombs of the saints was that those who loved them, seeing in what vicinity they lie, recommended to them those same saints as to patrons who ought to assist them by their prayers before God. Prayer rested on suffrages and satisfactions offered by the Church Militant. Our Lady, the angels and saints themselves present these suffrages to God and add to them the weight of their own merit, which increase the value many times over in the eyes of God. All three members of the mystical body are bound together.

Reflection: A family that prays together stays together. Always and everywhere, remember to pray for the Church Suffering!

Eternal rest grant unto them, O Lord, and let perpetual light shine upon them. May they rest in peace. Amen.

Accidental Glory

Pray constantly. — *1 Thessalonians 5:17*

"Always pray for the dead. If deceased persons are prayed for by offering the Eucharist or by any prayer and have no further need of purification, the prayers are not unavailing. The deceased in heaven receive an increase in their intimacy of God's love and an increase in their own intercessory power" — St. Thomas Aquinas, who called this "accidental glory."

Reflection: God is never outdone in generosity! No prayer is ever wasted. Pray, pray, pray.

Eternal rest grant unto them, O Lord, and let perpetual
light shine upon them. May they rest in peace. Amen.

Pray for Children

"Let not your hearts be troubled; believe in God, believe also in me. In my Father's house are many rooms; if it were not so, would I have told you that I go to prepare a place for you? And when I go and prepare a place for you, I will come again and will take you to myself, that where I am you may also be." — John 14:1-3

"If death has taken a child, or another dear one from you, and you are suffering intensely from this loss, wishing to be able to help, defend, aid and serve him, although there seems nothing further you can do — take note you can still find a way of assisting and aiding him in the person of the poor. Everything you give to the poor will truly benefit your dear deceased. By aiding the one you have lost, in the person of the poor, you will soon give him possession of eternal bliss" — St. Ambrose.

Reflection: Researchers verify that giving things away and helping others has a significant positive effect on our happiness here — and, I would add, in the hereafter.

Eternal rest grant unto them, O Lord, and let perpetual light shine upon them. May they rest in peace. Amen.

Joy in Purgatory

Henceforth there is laid up for me the crown of
righteousness, which the Lord, the righteous judge, will
award to me on that Day. — 2 Timothy 4:8

"Saved! What joy there is in the word. And this is indeed the song of purgatory. Saved! The soul has passed through the troubled waters of life, has been buffeted by the winds and waves of passion and temptation, and now it knows the great calm of being safely in port" — Archbishop Jean-Arthur Chollet, French author.

Reflection: The holy souls can never sin. They can never offend God again. Celebrate their eternal joy. Appeal to the joyful souls to preserve you from relapse into sin.

Eternal rest grant unto them, O Lord, and let perpetual
light shine upon them. May they rest in peace. Amen.

To Console and Be Consoled

*"May you be blessed by the Lord; for you have
had compassion on me."— 1 Samuel 23:21*

"By showing mercy toward the deceased, we satiate their hunger and quench their thirst; by paying their debts, we strip ourselves, as it were, of our spiritual treasures in order to enrich them; we free them from a slavery harsher than any imprisonment; we give these travelers the hospitality of heaven, of God's own home. When judgment day dawns, a chorus of voices will rise on our behalf, for those liberated souls will cry, 'This priest, this man, this woman ... helped us and freed us; he descended among us to extinguish the flames; he comforted us and with his suffrages opened for us the way to heaven" — St. Francis de Sales.

Reflection: Offer hospitality to others generously for the sake of your dearly departed.

---

*Eternal rest grant unto them, O Lord, and let perpetual
light shine upon them. May they rest in peace. Amen.*

DECEMBER 31

Do Not Forget the Departed

*Lo! I tell you a mystery. We shall not all sleep, but we shall all
be changed, in moment, in the twinkling of an eye, at the last
trumpet. For the trumpet will sound, and the dead will be raised
imperishable, and we shall be changed. — 1 Corinthians 15:51-52*

How important the redemption of the poor souls was for Therese Neumann shows in the bequest to her brother, Ferdinand: "Do not forget the departed. Pray every day for the departed, not only pray, but offer all difficulties coming on to you for the departed. As long as they are alive, we care for them and try to help them. Now, when they need our help, we usually don't think of them anymore. But they are waiting and need our help. They cannot help themselves. However, now, being in the next world, they are closer to us than ever before they could be when alive." And in an urgent manner she added: "Do not keep this, what I have said, for yourself, but tell all the people you will ever meet!"

Reflection: Never let a day go by without praying for the holy souls in purgatory. "May the Lord grant a peaceful night and a perfect end to us and to all our absent brothers and sisters. Amen." Pray the Prayer for a Happy Death (see page 392).

---

*Eternal rest grant unto them, O Lord, and let perpetual
light shine upon them. May they rest in peace. Amen.*

THE PASSING NATURE
OF ALL THINGS

There is a unique 100-year-old church on the banks of the Tiber in Rome called the Church of the Sacred Heart of Suffrage. The church has an elaborate French Gothic façade. It reminded Father Vittore Jouet, a French priest, of his beloved France.

Father Jouet erected this chapel to offer prayers for the dead. He traveled throughout Europe looking for relics or evidence of the suffering souls in purgatory. He placed these relics in his museum, which is located in his beloved Sacred Heart of Suffrage Church. Father Jouet died in 1912 in the museum, surrounded by his treasured collections.

The museum contains objects with burnt fingerprints of the souls begging the living for prayers, especially Masses. Remember, the burn marks on these relics are not from a physical fire but from the fire within, an interior burning for God. With each story there are three recurring themes: Purgatory exists; burning marks on items that point to the fire of an ardent burning for God; and the story of beloved ones, friends, and religious who urgently request Masses to be celebrated for their release.

The following are pictures of the most important relics of the holy souls to remind the faithful of the necessity of prayers for the dead and our own need for prayers when we die.

left: Façade of Parrocchia Sacro Cuore (Sacred Heart Parish) in Rome, Italy. Note the image of the holy souls in purgatory above the door.

below: Wall of Relics in the "Little Museum of Purgatory" at Parrocchia Sacro Cuore (Sacred Heart Parish) in Rome, Italy.

left: Louise LéSènechal asking her husband, Louis, for Masses, left as a sign the print of five fingers on his nightcap.

right: A burn mark made on the apron of Sister M. Herendorps, a lay sister of the Benedictine Monastery of Winnemberg, Germany, by the hand of deceased Sister Mary Clare Schoelers, a choir sister of the same order, who was a victim of the plague of 1637. The lower part shows the impression of two hands made by the same sister on a strip of linen.

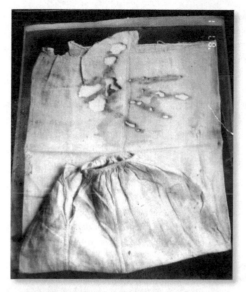

left: Right handprint made on the cut-off sleeve of the chemise of Venerable Mother Fornari by deceased Father Panzini, which passed through the tunic and left an imprint on the sleeve, stained with blood. Deceased Father Panzini (former abbot of the Benedictine Olivetan monastery in Mantua, Italy) was requesting Masses to be offered by the sisters.

left: Fingerprint left by deceased Sister Mary of St. Luigi Gonzaga asking her fellow sister, Sister Margareth, for prayers. She was in purgatory to atone for her lack of patience in accepting God's will in her final illness.

left: Left hand impressed on the table that Venerable Mother Isabella used for her work, by deceased Father Panzini. It is very clear and bears the sign of the cross cut deeply into wood.

below: Mark left on a copy of the book *The Imitation of Christ* by a deceased woman asking her daughter-in-law for Masses.

above: Fingerprints by deceased Joseph Schitz left on a prayer book. He was asking his brother for prayers to atone for his lack of piety during his life on earth.

right: A ten-lire Italian banknote left by a deceased priest who asked for Masses to be offered for him.

PRAYERS RECOMMENDED IN REFLECTIONS

Act of Contrition

O my God, I am heartily sorry for having offended you, and I detest all my sins because of your just punishments; but most of all because they offend you, my God, who are all good and deserving of all my love. I firmly resolve, with the help of your grace, to sin no more and to avoid the near occasions of sin. Amen.

The Angelus

V. The angel of the Lord declared unto Mary;
R. And she conceived by the Holy Spirit.
Hail Mary ...
V. Behold the handmaid of the Lord.
R. Be it done unto me according to your word.
Hail Mary ...
V. And the Word was made flesh,
R. And dwelt among us.
Hail Mary ...
V. Pray for us, O holy Mother of God.
R. That we may be made worthy of the promises of Christ.

Let us pray: Pour forth, we beseech you, O Lord, your grace into our hearts, that we, to whom the incarnation of Christ, your Son, was made known by the message of an angel, may by his passion and cross be brought to the glory of his resurrection, through the same Christ our Lord. Amen.

Chaplet of Divine Mercy

On ordinary rosary beads pray: Our Father, Hail Mary, the Apostles' Creed.

On the large beads for each decade pray:

> Eternal Father, I offer You the Body and Blood, Soul and Divinity of Your dearly beloved Son, Our Lord, Jesus Christ, in atonement for our sins and those of the whole world.

On the small beads for each decade pray:

> For the sake of His sorrowful Passion, have mercy on us and on the whole world.

Guardian Angel Prayer

Angel of God, my guardian dear, to whom God's love commits me here, ever this day be at my side, to light and guard, to rule and guide. Amen.

Hail, Holy Queen

Hail, Holy Queen, mother of Mercy, our life, our sweetness, and our hope. To you do we cry, poor banished children of Eve. To you do we send up our sighs, mourning and weeping in this valley of tears. Turn then, most gracious advocate, your eyes of mercy toward us, and after this our exile show unto us the blessed fruit of your womb, Jesus. O clement, O loving, O sweet Virgin Mary.

V. Pray for us, O holy Mother of God.
R. That we may be made worthy of the promises of Christ.

Memorare

Remember, O most gracious Virgin Mary, that never was it known that anyone who fled to your protection, implored your help, or sought your intercession was left unaided.

Inspired by this confidence, I fly unto you, O Virgin of virgins, my Mother; to you I come, before you I stand, sinful and sorrowful. O Mother of the Word incarnate, despise not my petitions, but in your mercy, hear and answer me. Amen.

Morning Offering

(Written in 1884 by Father François-Xavier Gautrelet. Recommended by St. John Paul II.)

O Jesus, through the Immaculate Heart of Mary, I offer you my prayers, works, joys, and sufferings of this day in union with the Holy Sacrifice of the Mass throughout the world. I offer them for all the intentions of your Sacred Heart: the salvation of souls, the reparation for sin, and the reunion of all Christians. I offer them for the intentions of our bishops and in particular for those recommended by our Holy Father this month. Amen.

Prayer for a Happy Death

(By Blessed John Henry Newman)

O my Lord and Savior, support me in my last hour by the strong arms of your sacraments and the fragrance of your consolations. Let your absolving words be said over me, and the holy oil sign and seal me. Let your own body be my food and your blood my sprinkling. Let my Mother Mary come to me, and my angel whisper peace to me, and your glorious saints and my own dear patrons smile on me; that, in and through them all, I may die as I desire to live, in your Church, in your faith, and in your love. Amen.

Psalm 130

"De Profundis"

(The Church uses this in the liturgy as the official prayer for the souls in purgatory.)

Out of the depths I cry to thee, O LORD!
    Lord, hear my voice!
Let thy ears be attentive
    to the voice of my supplications!
If thou, O LORD, shouldst mark iniquities,
    Lord, who could stand?
But there is forgiveness with thee,
    that thou mayest be feared.
  I wait for the LORD, my soul waits,
    and in his word I hope;
my souls waits for the LORD
    more than watchmen for the morning,
    more than watchmen for the morning.
O Israel, hope in the LORD!
    For with the LORD there is steadfast love,
    and with him is plenteous redemption.
And he will redeem Israel
    from all his iniquities.

Te Deum

You are God: we praise you;
You are the Lord: we acclaim you;
You are the eternal Father:
All creation worships you.
To you all angels, all the powers of heaven
Cherubim and Seraphim, sing in endless praise:
    Holy, holy, holy, Lord, God of power and might,
    heaven and earth are full of your glory.

The glorious company of apostles praise you.
The noble fellowship of prophets praise you.
The white-robed army of martyrs praise you.
Throughout the world the holy Church acclaims you:
Father, of majesty unbounded,
your true and only Son, worthy of all worship,
and the Holy Spirit, advocate and guide.
You, Christ, are the king of glory,
the eternal Son of the Father.
When you became man to set us free
You did not spurn the Virgin's womb.
You overcame the sting of death,
and opened the kingdom of heaven to all believers.
You are seated at God's right hand in glory.
We believe that you will come, and be our judge.
Come then, Lord, and help your people,
bought with the price of your own blood,
and bring us with your saints
to glory everlasting.

Spiritual Communion

My Jesus, really present in the Holy Sacrament of the Altar, since I cannot now receive thee under the sacramental veil, I beseech thee, with a heart full of love and longing, to come spiritually into my soul through the Immaculate Heart of thy most holy Mother, and abide with me forever; thou in me, and I in thee, in time and in eternity, in Mary.

Prayer of Daily Neglects

(A Poor Clare nun who had just died appeared to her abbess, who was pray-ing for her, and said to her: "I went straight to heaven, for, by means of this prayer, recited every evening, I paid all my debts.")

Eternal Father, I offer You the Sacred Heart of Jesus, with all its Love, all its Sufferings, and all its Merits.

First to expiate all the sins I have committed this day and during all my life. Glory Be.

Second, to purify the good I have done badly this day and during all my life. Glory Be.

Third, to supply for the good I ought to have done, and which I have neglected this day and during all my life. Glory Be.

What Is an Indulgence?

"An indulgence is a remission before God of the temporal punishment due to sins whose guilt has already been forgiven, which the faithful Christian who is duly disposed gains under certain prescribed conditions through the action of the Church which, as the minister of redemption, dispenses and applies with authority the treasury of the satisfactions of Christ and the saints.

"An indulgence is partial or plenary according as it removes either part or all of the temporal punishment due to sin. The faithful can gain indulgences for themselves or apply them to the dead" (CCC, n. 1471).

- For memberships, Perpetual Mass Remembrance, and to obtain Gregorian Masses, contact: Pious Union of St. Joseph for the Suffering and Dying, 953 East Michigan Avenue, Grass Lake, MI 49240; www.piousunionofstjoseph.org.
- To become a Spiritual Child of Padre Pio contact: National Center for Padre Pio, 111 Barto Road, Barto, PA 19504; www.padrepio.org.
- Association of the Miraculous Medal, 1811 West Saint Joseph Street, Perryville, MO 63775-1598; 1-800-264-6279; www.amm.org.
- National Shrine of the Divine Mercy, Eden Hill, Stockbridge, MA 01263; 1-413-298-3931; www.thedivinemercy.org.

BIBLIOGRAPHY AND
ACKNOWLEDGMENTS

Alberione, Blessed James, S.S.P., S.T.D., *Lest We Forget*, St. Paul Editions, Boston, MA, 1967.

Alighieri, Dante, *Divine Comedy*, translated by Allen Mandelbaum, Everyman's Library, New York, 1995.

Anderson, Gary A., "The Current of Creation: The Jewish Sources of Christian Charity," *Commonweal*, September 27, 2013.

Anderson, W. H., S.J., *Purgatory Surveyed*, Burns and Oates, London, 1874.

Apostoli, Father Andrew, C.F.R., *Fátima for Today, The Urgent Marian Message of Hope*, Ignatius Press, San Francisco, 2010.

Arminjon, Father Charles, translated by Susan Conroy and Peter McEnerny, *The End of the Present World and the Mysteries of the Future Life*, Sophia Institute, Manchester, NH, 2008.

Ball, Ann, *Catholic Book of the Dead*, Our Sunday Visitor, Huntington, IN, 1995.

Balthasar, Hans Urs von, "Purgatory," *Magnificat*, November 2009.

Biver, Comte Paul, *Père Lamy*. TAN Books and Publishers, Rockford, IL, 1973.

Brown, Beverly H., *The Little Flowers of Saint Francis*, Image Books, Doubleday, New York, 1958.

Buckley, Father James B., F.S.S.P., *Purgatory*, The Priestly Fraternity of Saint Peter, Elmhurst, PA, 2001.

Buehrle, Marie C., *I Am on Fire, Blessed Mary of Providence*, Bruce Publishing Company, Milwaukee, WI, 1963.

Catherine of Genoa, St., *Purgation and Purgatory, The Spiritual Dialogue*, translated by Serge Hughes, Paulist Press, Mahwah, NJ, 1979.

Catherine of Siena, St., *The Dialogue*, translated by Suzanne Noffke, O.P., Paulist Press, Mahwah, NJ, 1980.

Cloquet, The Abbé, *Month of the Dead*, translated by a Sister of Mercy, Benziger Brothers, New York, 1900.

Congregation of Marians, *Diary of Saint Maria Faustina Kowalska*, Marian Press, Stockbridge, MA, 1987.

Crosby, Michael, O.F.M. Cap., *Solanus Casey, The Official Account of a Virtuous American Life*, The Crossroad Publishing Company, New York, 2000.

"Dialogues of Pope St. Gregory" in *The Fathers of the Church*, Fathers of the Church, Inc., New York, 1959.

Esolen, Anthony, "The Most Abandoned Soul," *Magnificat*, November 2013.

Faber, Father Frederick, *All for Jesus*, TAN Books and Publishers, Rockford, IL, 2009.

Father Gabriel of St. Mary Magdalen, O.C.D., *Divine Intimacy*, TAN Books and Publishers, Rockford, IL, 1996.

Faure, Rev. Father H., S.M., *The Consolations of Purgatory*, translated by W. Humphrey Page, Benziger Brothers, New York, 1912.

Garrigou-Lagrange, Rev. Reginald, O.P., *Life Everlasting: A Theological Treatise on the Last Four Things — Death, Judgment, Heaven, Hell*, TAN Books and Publishers, Rockford, IL, 1952.

Gertrude, St., *The Life and Revelations of St. Gertrude the Great*, TAN Books and Publishers, Rockford, IL, 2002.

Guanella, St. Louis, *On the Tomb of the Deceased*, Pious Union of St. Joseph, Grass Lake, MI, 2010.

Haynes, Rev. Scott A., S.J.C., *Mystical Theology of the Mass*, Biretta Books, Chicago, IL, 2015.

Hubert, Father, O.F.M. Cap., *The Mystery of Purgatory*, Franciscan Herald Press, Chicago, IL, 1975.

Jugie, Martin, *Purgatory*, The Newman Press, Westminster, MD, 1949.

Kempis, Thomas à, *My Imitation of Christ*, Confraternity of the Precious Blood, TAN Books and Publishers, Rockford, IL, 1952.

Keppler, Rev. Paul Wilhelm von, *The Poor Souls in Purgatory: A Homiletic Treatise*, B. Herder Book Company, St. Louis, MO, 1923.

Lacordaire, Father Henri-Dominique, *Letters to Young Men*, Art and Book Company, London, 1902.

Lewis, C. S., *A Grief Observed*, Saber & Saber, London, 1961.

———, *Mere Christianity*, G. Bles, London, 1952.

Liguori, St. Alphonsus, *Preparation for Death*, TAN Books and Publishers, Rockford, IL, 1982.

Martin, Ralph, *The Fulfillment of All Desire*, Emmaus Road Publishing, Steubenville, OH, 2006.

McEachern, Patricia A., Ph.D., *A Holy Life: St. Bernadette of Lourdes*, Ignatius Press, San Francisco, CA, 2005.

Mechthild, St., *Meditations From Mechthild of Magdeburg*, edited by Henry L. Carrigan, Jr., Paraclete Press, Brewster, MA, 1999.

The Month of the Holy Souls, Vail-Ballou Press, Binghamton, NY, 1939.

More, St. Thomas, *The Supplication of Souls*, edited by Sister Mary Thecla, S.C., The Newman Press, Westminster, MD, 1950.

Mother Mary of St. Austin, Helper of the Holy Souls, *The Divine Crucible of Purgatory*, revised and edited by Nicholas Ryan, S.J., P. J. Kenedy & Sons, New York, 1940.

Nageleisen, Rev. John A., *Charity for the Suffering Souls*, TAN Books and Publishers, Rockford, IL, 1982.

O'Sullivan, Father Paul, O.P., *Read Me or Rue It*, TAN Books and Publishers, Rockford, IL, 1992.

Parente, Father Allesio, O.F.M. Cap., *The Holy Souls, "Viva Padre Pio,"* National Center for Padre Pio, Barto, PA, 1994.

Petrisko, Thomas W., *Inside Purgatory*, 2000, St. Andrew's Productions, McKees Rocks, PA, 2000.

Potter, Venerable Mother Mary, *Devotion for the Dying*, TAN Books and Publishers, Rockford, IL, 1991.

Ratzinger, Joseph Cardinal (Pope Benedict XVI), *God and the World: A Conversation with Peter Seewald*, Ignatius Press, San Francisco, 2002.

———, *The Ratzinger Report: An Exclusive Interview on the State of the Church*, Ignatius Press, San Francisco, 1985.

Renè-Bazin, Marie, *God's Threshold: Purgatory*, Clonmore and Reynolds, Dublin, 1957.

Rolheiser, Father Ronald, O.M.I., "Purgatory: Seeing the Fullness of God for the First Time," *Catholic New World*, November 18-December 1, 2012.

Sheen, Fulton J., *Manifestations of Christ*, National Council of Catholic Men, Washington, DC, 1932.

———, *The Moral Universe: A Preface to Christian Living*, Bruce Publishing Corporation, Milwaukee, WI, 1936.

Taylor, Michael J., S.J., *Purgatory*, Our Sunday Visitor, Huntington, IN, 1998.

Teresa of Ávila, *Interior Castle*, Ave Maria Press, Notre Dame, IN, 2007.

The St. Gregory Hymnal and Catholic Choir Book, Singers' ed., Melody ed., *Languentibus in Purgatorio*, St. Gregory Guild, Philadelphia, 1920.

Thérèse of Lisieux, *Story of a Soul: The Autobiography of St. Thérèse of Lisieux*, translated by John Clark, O.C.D., ICS Publications, Washington, D.C., 1972.

Ursuline Nun of Sligo, Ireland, *30 Days for the Holy Souls, Stories About Purgatory and What They Reveal*, TAN Books and Publishers, Rockford, IL, 1992.

Vaughan, Right Rev. Mgr. John S., *Thoughts for All Times*, Little Flower Press, Front Royal, VA , 1998.

ABOUT THE AUTHOR

SUSAN TASSONE has long been a passionate champion for the holy souls in purgatory and is recognized as leading the "purgatory movement" in the world. She's the author of five best sellers, and her first work, *The Way of the Cross for the Holy Souls in Purgatory*, has sold more than 85,000 copies. (Her other books are: *Praying with the Saints for the Holy Souls in Purgatory; Prayers, Promises, and Devotions for the Holy Souls in Purgatory; The Rosary for the Holy Souls in Purgatory; St. Faustina Prayer Book for the Holy Souls in Purgatory;* and *Thirty-Day Devotions for the Holy Souls.*)

Susan continues to work tirelessly to raise donations for Masses for the holy souls, and she is a popular speaker and frequent guest on radio and television shows.

In 2013, Susan was featured in the groundbreaking documentary *Purgatory: The Forgotten Church.*

She holds a master's degree in religious education from Loyola University and is a consultant for a major nonprofit philanthropic organization. Susan had the honor and privilege of being granted two private audiences with St. John Paul II, who bestowed a special blessing upon her and her ministry for the holy souls.

Her website is: www.susantassone.com.